May 2012

SPIRITUAL FRIENDSHIP

Tom

We've been slugging it
out in the trenches
over a lot of years
Grateful for you

Norm

SPIRITUAL FRIENDSHIP

*The Art of Being Friends With God
and a few Others*

NORM ALLEN

CLEMENTS PUBLISHING GROUP
Toronto

Clements Publishing Group Inc.
6021 Yonge Street, Suite 213
Toronto, Ontario
M2M 3W2 Canada
www.clementspublishing.com

Edited by Karen Stiller
Cover Design by Greg Devitt

Library and Archives Canada Cataloguing in Publication

Allen, Norm, 1947–
Spiritual friendship / Norm Allen.

Includes bibliographical references.
ISBN 978-1-926798-08-0

1. Friendship—Religious aspects—Christianity. I. Title.

BV4647.F7A44 2012   241'.6762   C2012-901377-3

CONTENTS

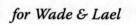

for Wade & Lael

CHAPTER 1

BEING FRIENDS WITH GOD
AND A FEW OTHERS

"What I find hard to believe is that all 5000 people forgot their lunch—except one little boy."

Those words from a man I already found annoying. I had just shared what I thought were carefully crafted insights from one of the most compelling stories in the Gospels—Jesus feeding the 5000. It was the first session of a weekend retreat of teaching and sharing.

I hadn't even wanted this guy invited to the retreat; he bothered me so much. Now this.

Then, the next morning, he had a profound experience with the God who loves him.

He became a wonderful contributor to our retreat as his dormant faith gained joyful expression. And now, when I look back, I realize he actually had a pretty good point about the kid and his lunch.

For the last 15 years he and I have become companions in our faith journey. He has contributed deeply to my life and work, as we have shared friendship through his dark times with health, family and business challenges.

I have found friendship that connects at the deepest spiritual place in the strangest and most unexpected ways. That friendship is one of them.

I am in the business of friendship, and have been for the last quarter century. My work has taken place mostly among strong-minded men and women who own, operate, manage and control enterprises in business, professional and faith-based sectors of our marketplace.

I could be described as the founder, president or janitor of Touchstone Ministries. This charity was created by some friends who wanted to give me the freedom to just "be a friend in Christ" to marketplace people.

Our mission statement is to offer, encourage and teach friendship in Christ among leaders in the business, political, arts and spiritual marketplaces. Touchstone's goal is to nurture an ever-expanding circle of friends who experience God's love, then love God in return, with their whole heart, soul, mind and strength, and express leadership that emerges from their identity in Christ.

In any given week I participate in regular groups that meet for prayer and friendship. I meet with individuals who have needs in work and family. I lead small retreats for reflection and listening deeply to God and one another.

In most cases I meet people by word-of-mouth references. When we first meet, there is the normal sniffing around to get trust levels up. Early on, I make it clear that even though I have a focus on following Jesus, I have no interest in imposing this focus on them. I listen more than talk, so my new friend may establish the boundaries for our conversations. Often, I'll suggest they think about what we've discussed, and if they'd like a second meeting, I'll leave it to them to initiate. When time and space is right in their journey they can invite me along.

This is a new kind of friendship. It is spiritual friendship. Surprisingly many of us offer this to one another intuitively, without necessarily knowing we are doing it.

Hundreds of people have made these discoveries along with me and have found health for their souls, their work and their friendships. They have been my teachers and guides as we have explored spiritual friendship together. The best stuff I know is what they have taught me. I'm still very much an explorer of friendship that connects in friendship with Jesus.

The energy for this work draws from my own hunger for a more authentic and real relationship with God in Christ—and to experience it in companionship with others who feel the same way.

Friendship that connects with and nourishes our inner journey with Jesus is a tricky thing to describe, let alone define. Those of us who are used to being in charge and in control are often limited in our capacity for self-reflection and self-knowledge. Our lives are strongly focused on making the deal, building the business, raising the money, managing the enterprise.

Our work fulfills our hunger to create, build and grow and more often than not, it is the core of our identity in the world. But vocational success—as wonderful as it is—can diminish our capacity for the softer things in life, like love and relationship with our spouses, children and friends. That is its danger.

The skills that contribute to our vocational success often are not the same as those that shape relationships. A friend once told me that his success as a lawyer meant he sacrificed family, friends and church relationships. In my experience he is no exception.

In quiet moments this imbalance concerns us deeply. But the demands of life and the expectations of our marketplace make it easy to ignore. So, we drive on.

The creation stories of our tradition, however one chooses to interpret them, are one of the key places we discover our holy longing for lives that are rich in accomplishment, but also rich in relationship with God and those closest to us in life. Our vocation as human beings is to work as partners in creation with the One who actually built into life the energy to produce, reproduce, create and build—not only business or enterprises, but families, loving communities, and great works of art and music. Then we are invited to enjoy the creation we have been given.

Debates about the creation stories in Genesis can keep us from seeing the power that is at work here—creative power in God, nature and humanity. However we arrived on the scene, we are fired with creativity. We are creative in relationship with the Creator and the rest of creation. I once read that we arrive from the womb with our fists clenched and the rest of life is a process of unclenching them. I resonate with that image.

Adam and Eve arrived in response to God's awareness that being alone is not good for anyone. But the confusion they created for one another through deceit and losing perspective on their relation to God and creation, was an early warning that life in relationships is no walk in the park. In fact, as we know, that particular couple ended up outside the park.

The creativity that empowers us to build marriages, families, communities, businesses, and explore science, can also be twisted in ways that are destructive to us and to others. And yet the creation stories are also full of life, light and hope. A world filled with fruitful nature, beautiful cosmos, and beloved humans got twisted early. Jesus works in us to restore the world to God.

This broken place is the doorway of invitation to find wholeness in ourselves, in our marriages and families and in close relationships. Friendship that nourishes the soul starts at this broken place in all of us. A friend of mine who reached that place said, "I came to a point where things were so broken that I could either end my life or reach out for help." Thankfully, he reached out for help from God, his spouse and a few friends.

"Find a friend or two that will encourage you toward love and reconciliation—doing good." This was the advice I offered in a brief homily to a young couple at their wedding. "When your spouse is being a jerk, you need a good friend who doesn't reinforce your resentments, but encourages you to build with patience."

We become unbalanced. We pour ourselves into our work, at the expense of building relationships. The God-planted creative energy that drives us is so stimulating and overwhelming, it can shut off temporarily—or completely—the voices in life that call for reflection and relationship.

It is so easy for us to take God-given gifts of creativity and focus them only on ourselves, our work, our needs and our grievances. Work is a core human activity, a partnership in stewardship of creation with God. But life is a process of discovering love and learning that it isn't all about us. We need help in this process of growth.

We are trained to be self-sufficient, highly accomplished individuals whose success is measured by external indicators, mostly economic. We have proven our worth if we reach a certain position, achieve a particular net worth, and receive public recognition. None of these things are destructive in themselves. But the drive we have to gain them rudely intrudes into our ability to listen to what is really going on in our lives and in the lives of those around us. I have heard this same story countless times, in my own life, and in the lives of the friends who have invited me to journey with them.

Imbalance can also strike our spiritual lives. It is far too easy to rely on books, speakers, preachers and celebrities to do our thinking for us, leaving us with no personal experience of Christ ourselves. For many of us, our inner pressure to produce and perform comes from a foundational belief that our identity and worth depends on our performance. We fear that our friends will think less of us if we fail. And we fear that God is like our friends.

The last thing we need to break out of this cycle is more things to do that will improve us, balance our lives or give us quality time with loved ones. We already have an inner drive that adds too much to our already existing to-do list. We don't need more.

Don't let this book add to your list. If it draws you to respond to God's gracious invitation to friendship and safety, then it will have accomplished its task.

Use this book as a tool to see this special gift that God gives us in our lives. I will suggest, from my experience, how to be more intentional about nurturing spiritual friendship with a few friends. What I have to say is not necessarily the best or the highest path to successful friendship, but it reflects the ongoing lessons I am learning from friends, wise spiritual guides past and present, and in the pursuit of being a friend of God and a few others.

The creativity God placed in us to be partners in his work, also includes a word called "Sabbath." Now, that word is freighted with all sorts of baggage—most of it negative.

God called the rest he took from his work "holy." We are called to join in partnership with God at rest, as well as at work. We find the work part easier, but the health we want—and need—is often found in silence, rest from our work and enjoyment of life with friends and family.

We know the polarities of work/rest, noise/silence, drive/stop, but if we are honest we will admit that we find the work, noise, drive energies most attractive and easier to engage.

Yet, Sabbath is a gift from God for us, his people. Jesus said Sabbath is made for our benefit—not as another obligation to fulfill. Your Sabbath may be a time other than Sunday, but it is a time different from work. God called his Sabbath holy. Even our recreations and vacations can be more like work than Sabbath. True Sabbath is time in which you connect alone or with friends to be filled, healed and renewed by God.

What does Sabbath have to do with spiritual friendships? Sabbath, among many other gifts, gives us some of the time we need to focus on our relationships.

"It is not good for a human to be alone," is another key ingredient found in the creation stories. We tend, by our work and leadership roles, to be lone operators at the core of our way of living. Yet we want to be connected at a deeper level. Often, we feel helpless to change.

My son Luke worked with the homeless of Toronto's streets and valleys for nearly 10 years. When people asked him what he did, he said, "I do what my Dad does, build friendships with people. It's just my people know they are broken and his friends have many more ways to mask their same brokenness." He was right.

Friendship that nurtures the soul begins in our broken places. These are the places where we discover we need help from God and a few friends. It is here we also discover the power of receiving, and not just giving.

Agape and *philio* are two Greek words that describe two important sides of spiritual friendship. Agape is the sort of love that we offer others by having their best interests at heart. Usually, there is a giver and a recipient. Usually, we are the givers. Givers remain in control. They are in charge of the process.

Philio involves mutuality of love. Each has the other's best interest at heart. The relationship grows in mutual giving and receiving. Most of us have many friendships in the agape category. Giving is the role we find most comfortable. It allows us to maintain control and operate from a position of power. But the real growth in relationships comes when they are mutual.

Mature friendship is evidenced by mutuality, not dominance and submission. Here is where I have struggled with many of Christianity's more popular methods of spiritual formation. I don't like the word discipleship. It implies a wise teacher and a weak learner. Real learning—for growing people—happens as disciples of Christ learn from him together, and from each other.

We are all disciples, learning from Jesus. We may have gifts that happen to place us as teachers within the family of God. But we are healthiest as teachers when we remember we are

also learners and can be taught by the smallest child or most
humble adult.

Jesus invites us to follow him. We are invited to lay down
our lives for a purpose greater than self-interest. We lose our
way when we forget we are all followers of the One who loves
us and gave his life for us. Following together creates plenty of
space for learning from one another. We bring different gifts
and wisdom to the communal table, but it is all in the cause of
being true disciples of Jesus together.

This journey to restful friendship cannot be done alone. We
happened because of love. The ongoing happening of our lives,
year following year, needs to be nurtured by the giving and
receiving of love in relationship.

True spiritual friendship swims against the North American
cultural stream of an economic value system which cannot
comprehend giving with no expectation of return on investment. We need truth-tellers in our lives to remind us that—first
and foremost —we are the beloved sisters and brothers of God.
He actually likes us! We do not have to prove anything to God.
We happened because of love. Love is the freedom we need to
finish life in one piece.

This journey takes us down a road marked Incarnation. It
has been a road of freedom for me—my very own underground
railroad from slavery. Incarnation is a complex theological term
that has earthy and wonderful implications. It tells us that the
truth of God's love for the world was expressed in skin and
bone in Jesus Christ of Nazareth. He lived and experienced all
of life as we do and has lived it wonderfully on our behalf.

Jesus transforms our understanding of our relationship with
God and one another. "I no longer call you servants, because a
master doesn't confide in his servants. Now you are my friends,

since I have told you everything the Father told me. You didn't choose me. I chose you. I appointed you to go and produce fruit that will last, so that the Father will give you whatever you ask for, using my name. I command you to love each other" (John 15:15-17).

He also said that we are his friends if we do what he commands us (John 15:14). We may bristle at the conditional sounding nature of this statement. How can this be friendship if it depends on performance?

I've sat with friends as we have listened to Jesus' words, puzzled and even resentful at the apparent quid pro quo he offers: friendship depends on obedience. But Jesus is commanding love for one another. Love begets love.

Jesus is so embraced by the Father's love, and obedient to the demands of love, that he offers us a place in that loving vortex. Jesus only understood his life in the context of the overwhelming mutually loving relationship he shares with the Father. It is not demeaning or calculated love. It includes us in his plans for the world. For me, at this point in my life, it also means I'm enjoying his friendship most deeply when I am doing what he would do: loving, forgiving, reconciling and carrying burdens. I express the qualities of good friendship the most when I imitate, in my own inadequate way, his manner of friendship. Jesus was no theoretician. He washed feet and served bread and wine. And he said that was what he wanted us to do for one another.

Spiritual friendship is about the freedom to love and give ourselves to one another, experiencing the friendship of God for us, as we serve one another. We are inside that loving space inhabited by Jesus. He commits himself to helping us do what he commands. He's not a distant God who just adds burdens.

Jesus invites us to get in harness with him, sharing the burden and learning from the One who is gentle and humble in heart.

Friends serve one another. We are the skin and bone in which God's Spirit chooses to express the divine love for the world. We flesh out this message of love for one another. This is where the hard work and the great joy are discovered. As our lives connect with Jesus, we are given opportunity to be servants of one another in love.

We have friends for many reasons. We need friends to get ahead in our career, build our business, get a good deal, share a sport or hobby, make a reputation and/or accomplish a great mission. But this sort of networking for purpose is not what spiritual friendship is about. Friendships that nourish the soul are very different. They begin with our own reflective life in times of quiet thought and prayer. They require a commitment to the time and energy necessary to truly be present to one another, for no reason other than listening to the rhythms of God's work in our lives.

The foundation is the desire that the truth be told to us, and through us. The foundational truth is that we are loved and that we love. We are freed to speak other truths that involve candour, accountability and our shortcomings, only if love is the foundation.

Love creates an atmosphere of trust based on confidentiality and confidence that we have one another's best interest at heart.

I continue to battle my own fear of admitting my need for help. I have used sarcastic humour and aggressive behaviour to keep people who love me at a distance. I spent much of my early adult life hiding. One of the few people who knew me well was Ted Smith, a high school classmate. We played golf and tennis, but also provided a forum for each other to explore life's big questions. Our backgrounds were very different. He was a nominal Anglican; within my faith community he would have been classified as one who needed to be "saved."

While my faith community wondered if I would ever start behaving like a good Christian, Ted freely and openly explored faith issues with me, without judgment. He became a companion on my journey of faith.

We lost touch with each other in our mid-university years and crossed paths serendipitously about 20 years ago. We had lunch and caught up on our careers. When I told him what I do for a living, Ted said: "I always knew you'd end up doing something that was about God." In those words was confirmation that this was a friend who knew me well.

My faith community, however, would not have thought I was good enough. They had no real understanding of my love and fascination for Christ. This friend thought I was just right already. Ted had no desire to convert me to anything. He heard what drove me. He had higher expectations for my life than almost anyone else. This experience was a profound lesson for me. I meet with many women and men who describe themselves as unbelievers, atheists, agnostics or simply not religious, yet who have profound spiritual journeys coming from roots in their own lives. Sometimes they just need help identifying their spiritual journey.

Fear of judgment, criticism and failure often prevent the open expression of our inner journeys, until an appropriate and safe environment is discovered. Then the floodgates open because we all want to be heard, listened to, and allowed to speak freely.

The true inner journey can be lonely until we find authentic, transparent companions. When we become intentional about our journey, those companions often pop up in surprising ways. This book will help you find your own.

CHAPTER 2

WHY WE NEED SPIRITUAL FRIENDSHIPS

One day I threw a punch in anger and in the process, I found the way to satisfy my soul's hunger for friendship with God and others. I was 21, newly married, and frustrated as hell at my inability to connect honestly with God or anybody else. I was one person inside and another outside. No one really knew me, least of all myself.

It happened on a Sunday morning right outside our church. As the congregation filtered out after morning worship, an angry confrontation shattered their cheerful chatter. I was in the middle of it.

One of my church friends challenged my integrity about an issue that he wasn't directly involved with, and in fact, was misinformed about. As a 21-year-old man I knew only one way to deal with aggression: more aggression.

The argument grew hot and loud. I decided the reasonable thing to do was swing at my accuser. A friend grabbed my arm, pulled me away and led me to my car, restraining me before even more damage could be done. The church folks stood still, shocked, watching this ugly scene unfold.

Susan, my new bride, broke the uncomfortable silence on the drive back to our flat by saying: "That was dumb." I knew that. But I was very embarrassed and full of pride. So I made things even worse by becoming angry with Susan. I don't remember if we ate lunch together, but I do remember that Susan left me on my own that afternoon. Communication shut down.

Turns out, my Baptist friend and my poor wife were not the only targets for my anger. That afternoon I said, "This may be it for us, Jesus. If you are real, you need to help me in my failure—I can't even control my temper in front of church after worship." Ironically, this day that I would rather forget, is the day that the door of grace truly opened for me for the first time in my life. In my embarrassment, failure and isolation, I returned to the story of Jesus. I was not even sure that I believed in God at that point in my life, but his Spirit was stronger than even my unbelief. I was drawn back to the story of the One who had quietly fascinated me all my life.

I turned to the gospel of Matthew in my desperation. Nothing really grabbed me until I hit what is commonly called the Sermon on the Mount. For me it became, "the Sermon in Our Flat"—a lifeline thrown to a failure in need of divine help.

Jesus' words—anyone can treat someone well who treats them well, but you really show you are a child of the Father when you do good to those who treat you badly—stopped me in my tracks.

For so long I had been wracked with fear and doubt that I masked with anger, aggression and acerbic humour. But that day I said, "Yes! Jesus if this is what you are about, then I want to follow you. If you can give me the power and motivation, the freedom, to live this way, then I will not walk away from the faith of my parents, my wife, my friends and my church."

I apologized to the guy I hit. I hope I apologized to Susan.

The journey of matching my inner desires with my outward behaviour continues. Here lies the great challenge for us—bringing the lives we express to the world around us into integration with the quiet spiritual journey that is also powerfully at work within us.

For many of us, the fear of admitting our need for help keeps people who love us at a distance. We put on a uniform, a way that we decide to present ourselves to others, and we are reluctant to allow others, even those who love us, to see our true selves.

Two friends joined my son Luke and me for a round of golf. One I only slightly know, but I find him charming and gregarious. As the round began, there was lots of jocularity. As the round continued, the conversations got quieter and more substantive.

On the drive home, I commented to Luke that my gregarious friend sure took a long time to calm down and get relaxed in conversation. Luke told me I was out of touch with reality. "You both were like two bull moose locking horns on the first tee to establish who was the alpha male," he bluntly said.

Any meeting of two people can be incredibly complex. Author Miroslav Volf, in his book *Exclusion & Embrace: A Theological Exploration of Identity, Otherness and Reconciliation*, writes that there are four persons present when two people meet. There are you and me—and we are joined by my perception of you and your perception of me. Volf takes it a step further in his recent book *Allah: A Christian Response*, arguing that there are actually seven people present in any meeting of two. The original four (you, me, my perception of you, your perception of me) are joined by my perception of myself, (which may be unrealistic), and your perception of yourself, (also perhaps not completely accurate). Then, he adds God as the final member of this group.

Volf hints at the difficulty we have in knowing one another at a deep level. Communication between two people is complex, requiring much awareness of what is going on under the surface of the encounter. I was a Procter & Gamble salesman after university, selling bulk shortening to the bakery, restaurant and institution market. I was taught to wear a suit and tie as my uniform, never a sports jacket, so my clothes did not distract from my message about the wonders of our shortenings in the kitchens and bakeries of my territory. My uniform did not make sense to me at the time, but it was the rule.

I still wear uniforms. When I am on a tractor blowing snow on a blustery day at our country home, my uniform is heavy coveralls, warm boots, big mitts and a toque. My neighbours would laugh at me if I dressed with too much style. A dark suit, shiny shoes, appropriate tie, polished face and neat hair is the uniform I wear when I host a large formal event in a hotel ballroom or conference centre. My beloved toque would not fit here. Inappropriate clothing would draw attention away from the message of the program.

Informal is my preferred uniform in most of my work. I feel it makes communication less confusing and me more approachable if I am not outfitted in a power suit. Underneath the uniform, however, I am still just Norm, a jumble of gifts, liabilities, hopes, fears, successes and insecurities. The uniform may keep the wind out, neutralize criticism and facilitate communication, but it tells you little about me as a real person.

What emotional or spiritual uniform do you wear? I spent much of my early adult life hiding in the uniform of the comedian and wisecracker. I remember visiting friends in Boston when they were at Gordon-Conwell Theological Seminary. I was early in my youth ministry life and still used sarcastic humour as a weapon. I tossed a wisecrack my friend Lorna's way, pointing out one of her foibles. She is a feisty truth-teller. "Norm," she said, "as long as you use your humour to take advantage of any weakness a person reveals, nobody will ever confide in you or trust you."

Lorna was right. I made a commitment that my humour would focus on my weaknesses and others' strengths. I have failed often. But that experience with a friend who loved me enough to tell me the truth, helped me begin to change out of my uniform of cruel sarcasm. Lorna had my best interests at heart and took a risk to tell me the truth. A few years ago, she remembered and commented on that experience. "We often laugh about that moment, but I want you to know I see you are not like that now. You hold the lives of others gently and it is wonderful how much people trust you," she said. Years ago, I heard her. And I tried my best to change.

One of my favourite uniform stories occurred many years ago when I spoke at an international conference of a lovely organization called Birthright International. Many friends have volunteered with the local Birthright chapter in our home area, offering unconditional love and support to women considering their options about continuing a pregnancy. Louise Summerhill, Birthright's co-president, opened the conference with a talk about "planting seeds of peace" in the angry and turbulent world of the abortion debate. I followed with my remarks, and when it was over I had an opportunity to chat with Louise.

I wanted to ask about a fax she had sent me for a legal release to distribute recorded copies of my speech. That fax had the name of a friend's law firm in the heading. I assumed she must have borrowed their facilities or, (male stereotyping at its best), worked as an assistant while doing her Birthright duties. She explained that she was actually a partner at the legal firm and a volunteer at Birthright. "So you must know my friend Ted Smith," I asked, confident that she would, because Ted was a leader in the firm. Louise explained to me that she not only knew Ted, but had also worked for him as a young lawyer.

When I described my long and good friendship with Ted (we had been high school friends), and his important leadership role in our work of encouraging friendship in Christ in the marketplace, Louise was taken aback. She said that she had no idea that Ted would be interested in "spiritual stuff." My less noble side could hardly wait for my next chat with Ted. I knew I could have some fun with him about his ability to hide his softer, spiritual side from his partners at the firm.

That opportunity came. I explained my connection with Louise and her role in Birthright. Ted could only say, "I had no idea she had any interest in this sort of thing – is she religious?"

I explained to Ted that this co-worker he had known for years was a thoughtful and intentional Catholic, who was equally surprised to discover that he was also a thoughtful and intentional follower of Jesus. Ted laughed and said, "I am going to have to have a friendly chat with Louise."

We can all relate to Ted and Louise's story. They weren't being deliberately dishonest about their faith. But in the world of a law firm they had to put on their lawyer uniforms to function competitively and competently among their peers and clients—inner journey stuff would be viewed as a distraction.

Our culture focuses on getting the job/deal/transaction done, and does not leave much room for exploring the person with whom we are dealing in any holistic fashion. We come to know each other mostly in our functional roles. This compartmentalization extends to our marriages, families, faith communities, neighbourhoods and public service.

My late and dear friend Blair Slade was a senior person at one of Canada's Big Five banks. We had been friends since our teens, but when I met him in his office he was polished, formal, his desk clean and his focus on his responsibilities clear. When our families were together, "Uncle Blair" laughed easily, loved to roughhouse with the kids and could never keep his shirttail tucked in. He was a good spiritual friend to me, to Susan and our kids. He cared about our whole lives as we did for him, Anne and their boys.

At a study I was leading a few months before his death, Blair connected deeply with the story of Jesus and his conversation with the woman at the well. He found it a wonderful guide to shape his manner of dealing with those he supervised. When I offered the eulogy at his funeral, I looked out at a sea of bankers from the chairman on down the executive ranks. I told stories of Blair's life, family and particularly his deep inner spiritual journey with Jesus. At the reception after the funeral, I was taken aback by the number of Blair's colleagues who said, "I always knew him to be a humane person who operated with high integrity. I had no idea he had this sort of spiritual interest."

Even more surprising, but joyfully so, was his sister's surprise when I told her a story of Blair's tears after a Touchstone event that focused on the plight of Toronto's street people. She knew him as a banker and a brother, but not as a person who cared about social justice. This is a sad, yet common parable about how disintegrated our lives often are. We work in one set of relationships, do public service in another, and love and laugh with our families in yet another.

Real spiritual friendship moves across the disintegration, to help the persona that operates in one world leak into the others. But it can only happen if we have friendship with God and a few others at the centre of our lives.

The real tragedy of many of our lives is that more often than not, far underneath all our public faces, a deep and thoughtful personal spiritual journey courses through our lives. It can find no safe and authentic outlet for its expression, because we do not feel safe.

In my early spiritual formation, I was trained to study and learn the theology of my Baptist tradition at my church. But my faith was also shaped by what I learned in my home. Our earliest experiences of faith, love and family can shape the cut, colour and style of the emotional and spiritual uniforms we wear later.

Early in life I witnessed the tension between private life and public life. My parents were very good and loving people, but very much of their generation. The attitude was, no matter how messy things got in our household, no one outside the family must ever know. Even then I knew there was something wrong with this approach. The seeds of a desire to live more transparently were planted back then. I needed to know that there was acceptance of weakness and messiness for those seeds to grow —not an obsession with creating the appearance that all was well, regardless of the reality.

I remember my mother telling me she was mortified to discover that I was the only child who refused to make a macaroni necklace at a pre-school Sunday School class. Apparently, my actions might have damaged the family name beyond repair.

"Be a good boy and do what you are told," seemed to be the primary message from home, church, school, sports and music. Even Santa Claus was in on it. "He knows when you are sleeping and when you are awake," after all. So remember, "Be good for goodness' sake!"

Anne Lamott, in her novel *Blue Shoe*, has a character express a fear that is common to many of us. "Things are going so well, I am becoming anxious that the other shoe is going to drop and bad things will happen." Her friend replies, "God's only got one shoe."

If we picture God just waiting for our vulnerable moments to drop a hobnail boot on us, our ability to live with any freedom or hope for the future is constricted. I listened to a friend wonder if a recent reversal in his life was God putting him over the fire on a skewer. We both laughed at the idea, but it's one that lurks in our subconsciousness to create fear and insecurity.

I have spent much of my adult life trying to get to know the God with only one shoe. My early images of God included a menacing character with large, heavy boots, poised to stomp on us at a moment's notice for bad behaviour, for having too much fun, too much success or enjoying too many of life's good things. That God does not exist. But this joyless God who does not much like us felt real to me. Maybe he feels real to you too. Think of the messages you heard as a child. Were you told to colour inside the lines? Were you challenged with "what will the neighbours think?" Were you reminded that God is watching?

We have many deeply rooted governors on our thoughts, expressions and spiritual explorations—a mother's voice, a father's expectations, our faith community's fences around the definition of truth—and fears of what people will think. And those are just a few of the restrictions upon us.

In the summer of 1995, I was involved in the Convocation of Prison Fellowship International (PFI). The Sunday morning before the conference began, some of us went to a morning service at the Falls Church in the city of Falls Church, Virginia. In the van on the way back to the conference, a visiting member of the PFI board pointed to a police car beside us marked Falls Church Police. "It is quite a church that has its own police force," she chuckled. When someone explained that the city and church shared the same name but not police departments, she was relieved. But the truth is, we do have our own type of policing. The religious authorities of Jesus' day had temple police. We have our own versions within our faith communities, overt and subtle.

Debates are often stifled, making an exchange of thoughtful ideas very difficult. Regardless of denominational tradition there are politically correct views in each of them. We do not encourage the free exercise of opinion that does not conform to accepted norms. Yet I regularly meet women and men longing for a safe place to explore ideas and issues. A place to be honest.

We've all had moments where our experience of life does not coincide with the prescribed beliefs, practices or behaviours accepted by our particular religious or social tradition. Our lives include many questions that don't fit the answers we have received. Sometimes the questions aren't welcome, even among our friends. A friend was telling me how much she enjoyed Francis Collins' book *The Language of God*. I hadn't read it yet, so was interested in her explanation of his idea that science is God's language—concluding that evolution is consistent with his faith in Christ. When I told her that sounded good to me, her relief was palpable: "I can't talk about this with my friends at church - they think I'm not a Christian if I think this way," she said.

Instead of welcoming her consideration of new ideas about life and God, she found her friends afraid to think outside the prescribed thinking that they accepted as truth. There was no safety or capacity for growth among them.

Nicodemus, an early and secret follower of Jesus, was in a meeting of his political party committed to preserving their religion and their nation. The church police said, "We couldn't arrest Jesus because we've never heard anyone speak in this compelling way. It just didn't seem right." The chair of the council questioned their loyalty and asked, "Have any of our group gone over to his side?"

Nicodemus sat there, probably feeling shaken and divided, but nonetheless posed a thoughtful question: "Does our legal system allow us to condemn someone without even finding out the facts of the case?" This is not a question one ought to ask in this context, because in this situation, questions and idea exploration demonstrate weakness of belief and disloyalty to the cause. The chair attacked Nicodemus personally. "Are you from his crowd? If you only knew your scriptures better you wouldn't ask such ridiculous questions."

Political, social, moral and spiritual discussion still sounds a lot like this. Position taken. Attacks launched. Nothing learned. Much of my work is under the radar and behind the scenes, to create safe places for people to explore beliefs, ideas, passions and concerns without fear of being judged and dismissed because of their opinions.

Exploring a different spiritual path can be risky. Some people in positions of power are seen as strong and invulnerable. Letting people see what is going on at the spiritual, emotional level can jeopardize that image. Within marriages, such exposure can also feel risky. Spouses can be threatened when a partner of many years starts looking at life differently.

There is suspicion of religious people in parts of our culture. A friend's wife felt relieved after a dinner at our home. She was sure that someone like me would attempt to impose my beliefs on her. She kept waiting for the inappropriate religious behaviour to kick in. It didn't of course. I probably did other inappropriate things, but not the one thing that she feared.

On many levels, our image is our public identity. Until we are ready to present a new face to our world, we need private, safe places to explore where we may be going. It may not be right, but it is reality. Nicodemus and Joseph of Arimathea operated that way with Jesus. He was patient with it all.

Many times I have had breakfast with a friend who pours out an amazing story about the challenges they face in business, family, marriage or personal demons. The cry for help and support is loud, and the hunger for friendship, support and divine help is obvious and deep. The same person, the next day, in a larger group may be a completely different person. Someone asks, "How are things going?" and the response is, "Just great, a few of the normal challenges but just great." This no longer surprises me.

My friends are exercising their legitimate right and responsibility to determine who hears their story and knows what is truly going on in their lives. Discretion is necessary. They have sought out a safe place to be absolutely transparent. And transparency somewhere is absolutely necessary.

I have seen friends share serious health concerns with me but hide them from other friends—"They'll find out in the market I work in and think I am damaged goods. It'll be bad for my business career." Other friends feel worn out and at the end of their rope, but they don't feel they can let anyone know. "It might get out and be misunderstood and clients and investors would lose confidence in me," they say.

Our journeys go underground, sometimes for good reason, but almost always to our detriment. We need friends on this underground journey to explore what the Holy Spirit might truly be moving us toward. We desire change and the courage to make change—but change can seldom be done alone.

Somehow, Nicodemus discovered that another party member was on a similar private journey. We know this because we next see Nicodemus after Jesus' death, helping his friend Joseph of Arimathea remove the body of Jesus from the cross. They provide a proper burial for this controversial teacher; a heroic and risky act—thumbing their noses at the system—but the right thing to do at the right time.

Many of us are on a journey to escape spiritual claustrophobia, to fight the thought police, and find our true voice. Thomas Merton in his book *Spiritual Direction and Meditation,* describes being a spiritual guide as acting as "God's usher." Merton had no desire to tell a person what God may be saying to them, but rather offered to guide them to a place where they can hear God's message themselves.

I have needed spiritual friends. They are God's ushers in this journey to freedom and love.

CHAPTER 3

THE NOURISHING NATURE
OF SPIRITUAL FRIENDSHIPS

Spiritual friendship is friendship that nourishes our inner journey. It is a way of living in companionship with Christ—and a few other people—in which listening to the movement of the Holy Spirit in one's life is understood and confirmed by conversation with people you trust and with whom you can be completely transparent.

Spiritual friendship is not just about things we traditionally identify as spiritual: worship, prayer, study of holy texts and mystical reflection. While it may include them, it is grounded first and foremost in the earthy and broken nature of a world longing for wholeness. It is grounded in the truth that as long as Jesus is present in you, and I do not reject your friendship, I have the opportunity to stay in connection with Jesus through you.

Spiritual friendship is not about discipleship; at least, not as discipleship has traditionally been understood in Christian circles. Discipleship makes me think of absolutism, controlling accountability, and top-down teaching, among other things. One person discipling another implies that someone's got it all together, and someone hasn't. Spiritual friendship is different.

Jesus tells his disciples they are not servants but friends. He says they are to love one another and so demonstrate their connection with him. He teaches that we are to serve, to give our lives for our friends—the very reverse of imposition and exercise of power. Friendship provides the context for love to grow. It is then that the partners, or group, can stay together in love, even when the mission becomes costly and demanding.

"Lay down your life for a friend," is Jesus' yardstick for love between friends. Often we identify this with his extreme sacrifice on the cross, but not with his patience for kids in his lap, the slow uptake of the disciples, or encounters with the sick and needy.

In fact, we are rarely asked to take a bullet for a friend. But, would we consider laying down our agenda, our need to fix and control, for our friend? Real friendship emerges from trust. Trust is built over time. The ability to listen, accept and question, but not impose an agenda are significant nutrients in that growth.

Martin Marty, in his book *Friendship*, opens with the line: "We have friends or are friends, in order that we don't get killed." That gets your attention. Our survival in a healthy life depends on relationships. The health of our spiritual lives depends on spiritual friendships.

A friend asked me to a retirement party as his career ended. He had made it to the top of a large international corporation. At his party, all his peers and subordinates said wonderful things about his contribution to the firm. They said they would invite him back to consult. They even paid him a handsome monthly retainer just to be available.

When we had lunch a few days later, my friend said: "Well that's the end of the hockey tickets and the relationships. They'll never call me back. Once you are gone from your role, you are gone." His words proved prophetic. He became another lonely casualty of friendships based on corporate relationships.

My friend's colleagues weren't being disingenuous. Retirement parties are like the last day of summer camp: lots of expressions of affection and promises to write. But it rarely actually happens. If we want friends for life, there has to be more to our relationships than companies, causes and mutual benefit.

Spiritual friendship is higher and deeper than causes or businesses. I spend a lot of time supporting small groups of friends to continue to grow in relationship with one another—without any other rationale for their existence as a group. We often feel more safe connecting with one another when there is some obvious external reason for connecting—helping the poor, saving the narwhals—but a measurable output can get in the way of friendship. Spiritual friends must learn to just be, and not always do.

It is easy for groups to stay together by having a study focus or a shared project. Such things can be positive, but often they distract from the hard work of building friendships that nourish the soul. Creating opportunities for truly listening to what is happening in our inner lives is the most important role for groups committed to spiritual friendships.

Setting aside the agenda of having pre-determined conversation topics or study themes means that listening and being present to one another is more important than the content.

This freedom and space triggers many profound conversations. That does not mean we are set adrift on an empty ocean of talking about nothing. The conversations must include some listening to the stories of Jesus, or other words from God, to prevent the group from being narcissistic. Caring and listening can easily become a self-congratulatory process, rather than stimulation to mutual love and growth in spiritual journey.

Presence is more important than words. Some of us always want to tell our story, give our opinion, offer our advice. But, more often than not, what we truly desire in our lives is the presence of another sensitive to what is going on in our lives. Our wired culture makes it hard to be truly present to anyone. We have the buzz of a message or a call during lunches and appointments and even, sacrilege of sacrileges, on the golf course. We have to contend with Twittering about what we're having for lunch or the putt we just sank. It's hard to stay in the present with a friend when we are so mentally connected to other distractions.

There is a remarkable difference between being together and truly being present to one another. Spend a few moments listening intentionally to conversations around you, or the one you are engaged in. Are we listening to hear and learn? Are we listening to find a weakness in what our friends are saying, so we can prove them wrong? Are we waiting eagerly to correct or defeat the argument? Are we just waiting to get our next thought or comment into the mix?

Or are we patiently listening to more than just the words being said? Are we attentive to the body language, the emotional intensity, the joy and pain that shapes the conversation?

The only way we can be deeply connected at a spiritual friendship level is through significant commitment to presence.

A key to truly being present is to have only the best interests of your companion foremost in heart and mind. Too often, socialization in our culture leads us to the opposite.

This is another lesson we have learned over the years: circles of friendship are an act of societal non-compliance. In our culture we connect to gain advantage, influence, a deal, or to convince the other of our point of view. Doing so is frequently very selfish—we need friends to get ahead. We network for personal advancement. The irony is that we really need to be friends with others to grow *out* of our self-focus. Spiritual friendships are an amazing opportunity for our own growth— if we do not have our own growth as the objective.

Making contacts, or some variation of personal advantage, is a high motivator for many of us to build relationships. But they are not friendships that will develop spiritual depth if that is where they stay.

In 1988 my wife Susan and I were part of a group that came together around a particular issue in the congregation and denomination with which we were affiliated. We decided that it was best for us to leave and start a new congregation. What a disaster. Our group was united in the leaving, but not in love for one another. We were united in why we did not want to stay where we were, but had no clear unity about what we were building, or the level of commitment we had to each other.

All the competing agendas bubbled under the surface of the talk about divine guidance and our fellowship with one another. Our very thin veneer of civility shattered easily.

This is also true in our culture; we move from charming and amiable to angry and difficult quite quickly, if the opinions or strategies of the group we are with don't go our way. Spiritual friendship works through those issues. Spiritual friendships have the capacity to say that our relationship with Jesus is a higher unifier than our commitment to a particular cause, belief, political or social position. This sort of work in diversity makes for real growth and genuine love.

True friendship that has the capacity for spiritual growth takes a lot of work. It is much more than enjoying golf, food, mission trips, fundraising campaigns or business deals. These projects may bring us across another's path, and we may even sense that there is more possible in the relationship than what is seen. But if all we see is more personal advantage instead of the opportunity for the development of candour and love, the relationship is destined to go only so deep—not deep enough for spiritual friendships.

Spiritual friendships may even take us into relationships we would not have guessed possible. Availability is better than affability. There are many people who are attractive, fun to be with, and intense in their expressions of friendship. But when the chips are down they aren't available.

I remember the morning my father died. I was about to have my morning coffee when there was a voice at the porch door, "Anyone up? I have muffins for breakfast." My friend Gary did not even know that my dad had died. He just knew I would have spent most of the evening before at the hospital. He came to offer friendship in a tense time and became the first person I told about my dad's death.

Affable is great. Available is even better.

Circles of spiritual friendships have no agenda but friendship, authenticity and confidentiality. This is where the fruit of the hard work is seen. As one or two, or even more, begin to connect with one another with friendship and spiritual growth the only items on the agenda, a few things become clear.

First, these types of friendships are about friendship with God and a few other people in order to listen to God's moving in each other's lives. Anything else becomes a distraction and can damage relationships. Years ago, Touchstone had a wonderful group of men meeting regularly for breakfast in downtown Toronto with this kind of focus. A new fellow, who was going through some personal and business challenges, joined the group. He was tentative and cautious. It turned out, he had reason to be. He disappeared in a hurry after members of the group called to offer their consulting services to help with his business problems. They violated the purpose of the group, making it uncomfortable for him to return. "I thought I was coming to a safe place, but it didn't turn out that way," he said.

The capacity for authenticity is reduced when agendas get mixed. Trust is based on not taking advantage of someone's needs. Absolute confidentiality is required.

A group of us were having dinner one night. I was the professional exception in the group – the rest operated construction companies or sold equipment to the industry. We had been meeting from time to time, to chat about friendship. In the middle of dinner, one of the men said, "Do you realize we have known each other for many years, and this is the first time we have talked about these sorts of things? All these years we have operated at the surface, had fun, but never really known each other."

Men who normally competed with each other were working hard to leave those agendas out of what they did together when they were discussing life. It was a good thing.

John, the Gospel writer, quotes John the Baptizer describing the nature of his relationship with his cousin Jesus: "God in heaven appoints each person's work. You yourselves know how plainly I told you that I am not the Messiah. I am here to prepare the way for him—that is all. The bride will go where the bridegroom is. A bridegroom's friend rejoices with him. I am the bridegroom's friend, and I am filled with joy at his success. He must become greater and greater, and I must become less and less" (John 3:27-30).

The measure of friendship for John was "joy at his success." This is a simple way to discover how your relationship may be developing with someone.

Do you have real joy and pleasure with someone else's recognition and success?

If this joy is not present, there is work to be done. Competition that leaves us envious does not grow a spiritual friendship. Our culture is so performance and outcome-based that we define ourselves by our success. We find our security in accomplishments. Competition with one another for market share, attention and deals, or whatever is our work, drives us to achieve.

Celebrating someone else's success depends on us not being competitive at a basic level. Someone else's success does not diminish me, or my achievements. Recognizing an inclination to envy is a difficult moment in our spiritual journeys. When I am envious of another's success I know I am not secure in my own sense of identity and calling.

The next step is finding meaning and pleasure in someone else's success. John the Baptist knew his calling and knew his role in life. He knew what was important, and Jesus said that he was the greatest human being. John's whole life was built around pointing away from himself and toward another. The day he saw Jesus walking by, he said to some of his followers,

"There is the Lamb of God." He watched them walk away from him and follow Jesus (John 1:29,35).

John took joy in this role, satisfied that his job was done well. John's example has plenty of application in many areas of our lives, but the ability to set aside our own drive for personal success is very important if friendship is our priority. Discovering the joy that comes from watching someone else achieve recognition, success and praise does nothing but expand our own capacity for love and generosity.

Ron Nikkel, president of Prison Fellowship International (PFI), is my closest companion in Christ. We work in very different worlds. But we are committed to helping one another in our journeys with Jesus. I attended a PFI convention in Bulgaria where Ron gave a speech. He was wildly applauded for both the speech and his life's work. I sat in the audience and listened to my good friend being honoured. And I wept for the joy of it; me, who can so easily fall into envy and competition and feel diminished by another's success.

Jesus changes our understanding of the way we can relate to each other and to him. The God of the universe, who has chosen to be one of us, says he wants our friendship. And he wants us to do the same for one another. It frees us to not be diminished by our friend's happiness or good fortune, but to be blessed by the joy of it.

In his last hours with his friends over dinner Jesus said,

> I no longer call you servants, because a master doesn't confide in his servants. Now you are my friends, since I have told you everything the Father told me. You didn't choose me. I chose you. I appointed you to go and produce fruit that will last, so that the Father will give you whatever you ask for, using my name. I command you to love each other. (John 15:15-17)

There is much richness in this passage. There is a startling mutuality. Yes, these men and women around the table were disciples and followers of Jesus. But Jesus forever changes the nature of the relationship.

He is still the only saviour in the group. But in the hours to come, he will demonstrate how much he desired their friendship. Here we see a proximity and mutuality that is often missing in the way we help each other in spiritual formation.

When we are spiritual friends, we move out of the cognitive and propositional approach that is often dominant in spiritual formation traditions.

I stayed at a Benedictine Abbey in Saskatchewan for a week. One morning, as I sat in my stall in the church awaiting morning prayers, Father James, my conversation companion for the week, walked by and handed me a scrap of paper. "No statement of doctrine or dogma can replace the experience of the living God," he had scrawled.

This is the intersection of spiritual friendship: individual and shared experience of the living God through creation, scripture, silent reflection on life experience—and the willingness and desire to learn from one another's experience. Spiritual friendship is not just about an intellectual understanding of the Living God. And it's not just playing golf together on the odd Saturday. In spiritual friendships, those two come together in a life-transforming way.

There is a lovely Celtic Prayer that summarizes some of these thoughts in a beautiful way.

Friendship Blessing

Beauty of friendship grow between us
Friendship
without guile
without malice
without striving.

Goodness of friendship grow between us
Friendship
with light
with wings
with soul sharing.

Be in the eye of each friend
of my journey
to bless and teach each one.

The eye of the Father be upon us
The eye of the Son be upon us
The eye of the Spirit be upon us
The eye of the Friendly Three
Be upon us forever.[1]

I think you will discover you already have many friends who have the desire and capacity to be a spiritual friend for you. When I ask men and women to describe the most recent friendship experience they can remember, I get several responses. A blank stare is one of them. Others will reflect on an event that happened with someone years ago. Very few are currently, consciously connecting with a few people on a spiritual level. But they could be.

---

1. This anonymous prayer is cited from Ray Simpson, *Celtic Blessings: Prayers for Everyday Life* (Chicago, Ill.: Loyola Press, 1999), p. 6.

Truth is not only stranger, but better than fiction. We long to be told the truth. But we want the truth to be offered with love. The hardest and strangest truth we all have to hear is, "You are loved." And Jesus not only loves you. He likes you.

A few years ago I was meeting with my friend Tarcia, my spiritual director, who helps me with my prayer life by listening and making suggestions from her vast experience. This day she asked, "What is your main motivation in life?" I told her that at the end of the day, I just want to have been useful to God and a few people. Her reply startled me: "That's not true. What's your real core motivation?" I answered, "To love God with my whole heart, mind and strength and to love those he brings across my path." I felt sheepish. She asked me why I didn't just say that in the first place. I was afraid to say it, because I know I will not live it perfectly. I know I'll fail so I don't want to be embarrassed by my failure. As we talked, I realized that my fear indicated that I did not really believe that I was loved by God. If I am loved, the fear of failure and embarrassment is irrelevant. I can't lose the love. I just have to keep living it.

Writer G.K. Chesterton once noted, "Anything worth doing is worth doing badly." This truth applies to love. I express love imperfectly. The love I receive from others is also imperfect. If I focus on the gap between perfection and reality, I will never enjoy love as it is. My relationship with Susan, my children, and my closest friends is the place I experience the love of the God I cannot see. Human love is flawed but rich. It will change and mature, but only if I freely—and imperfectly—love and treasure the love I experience, however flawed it is.

We need the truth-telling capacity of a wise friend to help us hear our true voice and remember our true position. We are beloved children of the loving Father, friends of the Son, Jesus and guided by the Spirit. We are loved and free to say that we want to love each one who comes across our path. We will and do fail miserably. But the desire is true.

CHAPTER 4

INSIDE A SPIRITUAL
FRIENDSHIP

Friendships are like bathing suits. You only get out of them, what you put into them. This is a variation of a line I picked up from some old comedian, but as I walk this friendship trail, I think it captures an important truth.

It's one thing to be a golfing buddy, a working friend, a friend on a cause—it is quite another thing to connect only and simply for the sake of one's soul and for the health and well-being of the other. But how does a friendship begin to connect at the soul/spirit level? Ideally, friendships work best when there is no desire to "get" something from the other. But spiritual friendships work best when there is an intentionality about the growth and development of the friendship for the mutual benefit of the friends.

When I consider those friends who are now my spiritual companions in life, the initial connection between us often happened almost by accident. However, it soon became clear that we shared some extra ingredient that might cause us to move beyond acquaintance into friendship. My friend Ron and

I met when we were both youth workers in Toronto. We worked at the opposite ends of the economic spectrum. Ron was with so-called troubled kids, and I with an affluent group of high school students.

At first that difference appeared to be a barrier. But it soon became a bridge, as we explored what was significant about each other's work. It also did not hurt that within the organization that employed us, we were both contrarian and independent. We developed an alliance. Our conversations soon progressed into areas of mutual concern. We discussed how we understood God, marriage and family, work, and the integrity of our mission and calling. While still having the capacity to party and play, we often engaged in what many might consider serious conversation.

Early in our friendship we roomed together at a conference. We had an experience that we often reflect on as a being the key that opened the door to deeper friendship. It was a conversation that carried on into the early hours of the morning. We talked about our marriages. We both acknowledged that often we invested more creativity and energy in reaching out to the youth we served, than we did in our relationships with our wives.

We were transparent about both our desire to do better, and our failures. Thirty years later, married to the same loving and forgiving spouses, we recall that conversation—that first early opportunity for transparency and mutuality—with gratitude. In a recent conversation, Ron quoted from the famous Jude benediction: "He is able to keep you from falling." I added the next line, "and to present you faultless in his presence." We noodled back and forth on this truth. We laughed at the unlikelihood of either of us being found perfect. We acknowledged that it is only in the life of Christ that faultlessness can happen. And yet we had just discussed how our friendship had been one of the keys to our survival in the respective ministry roles we play; Ron's—through a large international ministry with over 100 member countries, and mine, through a small attempt to serve a loosely connected web of relationships.

Our friendship continues as a more mature reflection of its early beginnings. Allow me to use this relationship as a template for you and your spiritual friends.

Early on Ron and I discovered a common desire to explore spirituality outside the traditional evangelical-personal-salvation-prescription to include the justice and equity that we both knew also flow from the Gospel. Our individual inner journeys followed many of the historic streams of spiritual formation that we found in the monastic traditions of reflection, solitude and silence.

On our own we have developed prayer and spiritual practices that nourish our individual relationships with God. We both have a hunger to learn. When we grow stagnant in our inner journeys we explore new ways to strengthen Jesus' presence in our lives.

As we explore our experiences of frustration and growth, they become resources, enriching our times together. We have patience for each other because we acknowledge our weaknesses. We respect one another because we know and trust our unique strengths. The spiritual practices we experiment with individually also become safe resources for enriching our times together.

I'll spend more time on these practices later. They have become central to our mutual discovery of the active presence of God in our lives.

We share common interests. Although Ron is a sailor, he now shares my addiction to golf. We have similar interests in music and art. We also just like to have fun together "hanging out." We share a passion for the Gospel and for expressing it through our leadership gifts and organizational responsibilities. We still worry about money, people, politics and all the normal ingredients of organizational leadership. We need to keep growing and changing in these roles. Dealing with our frustration and loneliness gives us much fodder for discussion, laughter and tears.

Our marriages have lasted into their fourth decade and we have a common interest in helping each other grow in our relationships with our spouses through hope, love and patience.

Ron left Toronto for Chicago and then on to Washington, D.C. as his opportunities for greater leadership grew. Even though I stayed put, we developed a common commitment to meet at least twice a year. Fulfilling this commitment took effort. In the early days of our long distance friendship, we would connect sporadically. Rushed conversations, easily distracted by other concerns, grew frustrating. Eventually, we realized it was important to be more intentional about establishing specific times for friendship.

A slogan from the old, goofy TV show "The A-Team" is, "I love it when a plan comes together." It has become our mantra when we get together because we have a commitment to go with the flow. We want first and foremost to block out time and space for one another. We let the needs of our lives, our current mental and physical states, and the leading of the Spirit determine the agenda for our time together.

Jesus defines friendship as laying down our lives for one another. Each comes with ideas about what the other needs, and about what we ourselves may need. Pushing those agendas onto one another is a barrier to real listening and engagement at an inner life level. We have to acknowledge and then surrender them.

We have faith that God is present in our times together, and that if we listen well to scripture, creation, our stories and emotions, an agenda for conversation and identifying needs will naturally emerge. Trust in each other and trust in the Spirit fosters freedom to let things emerge unforced.

As we spend time listening and playing, it quickly becomes clear that neither of us has achieved anything approaching perfection in any area of our lives. We have had good runs in our work lives, and have been fortunate to receive affirmation from our respective communities for the work we do. "But if they only knew what jerks we really are," is another mantra we have in our visits. We share a common experience of brokenness, failure, and insecurity that is on the table when we converse. It is easier to be transparent about my need for help when my friend is in the same boat.

My spiritual friend and I share a common experience of the grace and mercy of God in our brokenness, failure and insecurity. The light shines brightest against the darkest sky. That has been our experience in this shared journey of faith. It is important to remind one another of grace with the broken stuff, or else you can become depressed about failure. Loneliness and brokenness are doorways to friendship with God and a friend.

Alone, we may focus on the broken places and become immobilized. A friend can remind us that we are loved and forgiven. They point us to the path of renewal and freedom in Christ.

We share a common experience of accomplishment and success that brings with it pressure, tension and significant loneliness. It is at this point our friendship becomes even richer. Ron has led Prison Fellowship International from a few member countries to its current list of 114 member nations. He has met with heads of state and religious leaders of all stripes. He has established a significant record as a spiritual statesman, building circles of people who serve the needs of prisoners and their families on a global scale. My work is quiet and behind the scenes in our marketplace. We have been fortunate to see significant growth for our individual work as our respective careers have gained credibility.

We both still fear becoming the leader who stops growing and whose thinking grows stale. We do not want to become complacent or careless in our reputations. We know we may be more vulnerable to the temptations around money, sex and power than we have ever been. We realize we are at an age where passing our responsibilities to others with grace and freedom may be more difficult than the original building of our organizations. We know this about each other because we share deeply, honestly and prayerfully.

As the years have passed, we have been through many stages and levels of communication. We now have an unspoken structure for our times together that includes food, drink, prayer, listening and just being a bit goofy. Like any other highly driven pair of individuals, we have to disconnect from the frenetic pace to slow down and listen to one another and listen to God. Our own independent spiritual journeys draw from many sources and contribute to structuring our times together.

It is here that the mystery of what is called the Trinity is an important clue for me about spiritual friendship. Many of us still carry vestiges of a stereotype that God is angry and aloof. I now understand that the relationship of Father, Son and Spirit is actually a jumble of relationships—a dance of love and companionship between the three. The Orthodox tradition calls this dance *perichoresis*. It is relationship that is intimate, organic, intertwined and flowing. When God made us, it was for the purpose of including us in this existing atmosphere of love and relationship.

A friend recently told me that another take on *perichoresis* is making room for the other. What a great way to describe a healthy loving relationship. Even Jesus, in his obedience and self-denial, was never outside the dance of relationship. His powerful obedience came from knowing he was the beloved. His actions were an expansive expression of freedom within the circle dance of the Godhead.

A senior church leader who participates in a regular friendship retreat with a group I lead, said that we offer permission to find the way that works best for each one. He spoke of the safety created in those spaces and times in the group. We provide many tools for reflection and conversation, but offer freedom for each to choose what nourishes them best.

By creating space for the other to find freedom in Jesus' invitation to follow him, we encourage more obedience and sacrificial change. Space to grow and compassionate love create the space for exploration of new paths of change, sacrifice and obedience.

When we build friendships with one another, we mirror back to God the intention for which we are created: relationship with

God and our fellow human beings. Holy texts, creation, and even my conscience help me understand God.

At a deep and personal level, my understanding of God is enriched and clarified in relationships with others. I know I am loved by the God I cannot see, when I am loved by the people I can see.

Anything we have, accomplish or hope to leave behind as a legacy is only a gift from our gracious God. But understanding ourselves in the light of our limited knowledge of God is best done in a lifetime of conversation with a few trusted friends.

I was asked to explain my work to a group of clergy over lunch. As I explained my understanding of the value of developing relationships that have no agenda except friendship with God, there was bemused puzzlement expressed by one member of the group. "I never have an appointment that does not have an agenda – projects need to be funded, committees need leadership, tasks need to be accomplished in the church," this busy leader said.

For many of us, that is also our experience of the world of church—it is a place to serve and work, but not necessarily to be nurtured. It brought to mind a CBC radio documentary I heard recently about an experiment at a U.S. medical school over 30 years ago. The school invited anonymous men to donate sperm to a bank that would be used to artificially inseminate women who participated in the project. The key for the donors was guaranteed anonymity, and for the women the opportunity to bear children whether they had a partner or not. Now that the children of this experiment are adults, they have an understandable desire to know about their respective birth fathers, for many reasons, including genetic predisposition to physical and mental illness.

These adult children longed to know if they had siblings by other mothers. Even more poignant was their desire to know if their father ever thought of them, knew they existed or were willing to have a relationship with them. We have a spiritual genetic history that instills a longing in us to know if our Father ever thinks of us, knows we exist or desires to have a relationship with us. Formal theology does not help us on these core relational hungers. They are not questions of intellectual interest but questions of personal connection.

Spiritual friendship is the divine response to this longing for connection. It knits together our spiritual longing as an individual with our friend's same longing. But it is in the sharing of the longing in community that we experience an enhanced sense of the Divine Presence in all of life. C.S. Lewis wrote about this in *Mere Christianity*: "God made us: invented us as a man invents an engine. A car is made to run on gasoline, and it would not run properly on anything else. Now God designed the human machine to run on himself. He himself is the fuel our spirits were designed to burn, or the food our spirits were designed to feed on. There is no other." Throughout the history of the Church, there have been many efforts to help us experience what Lewis is describing. Catechisms, Church and monastic disciplines, preaching, study, prayer, charitable giving and service are just a few of the tools that have been employed to both constructive and destructive effect over the last 2000 years.

It is easy to make the disciplines the objective, and to forget that the reason a discipline developed was to nurture our relationship with Christ, not to add another performance burden. This is about the architecture of our souls. All the tools of the devotional life are only scaffolding. Once a building is completed, its internal structural integrity makes the scaffolding unnecessary. In our spiritual lives, as the internal presence of Christ grows and the life of prayer grows, the scaffolding of the tools becomes less necessary.

We do need intentional activity to nurture our relationship with the God who invites us to listen to him. But, if a particular discipline is not making you more aware of God's loving presence or invitation to grow, hold it loosely. What is helpful for a season may need to be replaced. Our inner journey with God has changed and matured. Just as with human friends, the things that nurture relationship with God change as the friendship matures.

The tools we need may change as we age and mature, but the goal of a deeper awareness of the life and presence of Jesus remains. Friendship connects at this intersection. As friends age and mature in friendship, the ways that allow for comfortable friendship change and grow.

I'll have some suggestions in the next chapters about how we can nurture spiritual friendship even within relationships that are relatively young. It is not rocket science. It is investing time with a friend for listening to each other's inner journey. It is no different in our relationship with God. It takes a good friend to give us the encouragement and courage to leave old practices behind that do not help with our soul's life, and move into freedom of a developed internal relationship with Christ.

A friend of mine recently described my role in his life as being a light bearer. He said that I hold the Christ candle and move into new and unexplored places to say to my friends, "Maybe it's over here."

CHAPTER 5

LOOKING FOR A
SPIRITUAL FRIEND

It is a challenge to identify spiritual companions and to think about putting into practice some of what we're discussing in this book. It can be risky to try to readjust the assumptions we have in certain relationships. But it can also be wonderfully rewarding. You may meet every day with your future spiritual friend, and you don't even know it.

What is your core longing or desire in moving more closely toward Jesus? Do you know anyone else who shares the same desire or dissatisfaction with life, and particularly their spiritual life as it is presently lived out?

A holy dissatisfaction can be a good place to find common ground with a potential spiritual friend—and then to explore ways that will satisfy it. If you find yourself critical or dissatisfied with whatever your source of spiritual nurture and guidance currently is, consider who it might be that you would be comfortable sharing these kinds of thoughts with. Get together and have a discussion with someone who you think might share your concerns, or at the very least understand them. Think about what you can do differently to become more constructively engaged in meeting with God.

This is not a bitch-and-moan session about some church leader or disappointment with "the Church." There is already more than enough of this sort of complaining going on. It is unproductive. But dissatisfaction with the status quo can be the first step in transforming it.

Spiritual friendship presents an opportunity to be responsible for your own life—in companionship with someone else—in order that you may serve and be patient with this messy thing we call the Church in its many various expressions. Our greatest calling is to love and serve, not to be loved and served by an organization.

It may feel risky to ask a friend to make spiritual journey a practical and intentional part of your conversations. Nonetheless, the early steps can be rewarding. It can seem artificial at first, but, in time, comfort comes.

When they lived in Vancouver, my son-in-law had a scotch and cigar night on his deck with some friends every couple of weeks. My daughter thought it was just a scotch and cigar night. But these young men were sharing life stories and faith journeys in a transparent and yet safe way. It was spiritual friendship. It worked.

If you have a fishing buddy, a shopping partner, a tennis friend—someone you see on a regular basis for recreation or non-work—you may discover that they also share your desire for conversation about eternal realities but have also been reticent to inquire.

Depending on your age and stage of life, you may have spent time with a friend—or different friends—chatting about marriage, family, or business stress. It may have stayed at a purely superficial or prescriptive level. Could it go deeper?

Think of the person you would trust with any secret success or failure in your life. That is another way of identifying a spiritual friend. Who would you turn to if you really needed someone to have your best interests at heart?

We often discover we have a spiritual friendship, after it has already started to develop. My best friendships on this level became spiritual friendships somewhere along the way. Our time together as friends gradually became more focused on the spiritual.

At one time in my life I was not taking responsibility for my finances in an appropriate manner. My bills and obligations seemed out of control. I thought there was no easy way out of my jam. So I did what many of us do, I avoided even looking at the bills, until I finally came to my senses and approached a friend for help.

It was like going to the priest for confession. My financial problem was a form of sinful irresponsibility. My friend listened carefully and unpacked the issues. He identified the worst case scenario. Suddenly, I was not afraid any more. I could face my responsibilities.

What made this a step in the spiritual friendship journey? First, it involved trust and confidentiality around an issue of pride and failure for me. I knew that my friend had my best interests at heart and shared my desire to follow Jesus with integrity. He recognized it was a serious, but not fatal situation. He helped me develop a solution.

The freedom I felt from just telling the truth about my secret was a powerful gift. Knowing my friend understood my failure—but did not add shame and judgment to his listening—added grace to what could have been fire.

Reflect on moments like that in your own life. Who have been the people present for you with grace and kindness in the tough times? Who do you think of when you have a quiet moment and say, "Boy, I'd like to spend more time with _____. They've got some qualities I value."

Who is your friend without an agenda? Who is free from the need to connect to the best people for their own advantage? Who are the people that you care to be a friend with, absent of making connections that might advance you and your own goals?

The flip side of this is your own capacity and interest for being present to others. Who comes to you for safe advice or exploration of ideas and questions? My friend Greg and I have been meeting occasionally to foster this sort of spiritual companionship. He lives in Vancouver and would like to find a spiritual companion closer to home. Greg shared with me that a friend was having a tough time, and opened up to him in a way he had never done. I agreed with Greg that his Vancouver friend was one of the most self-contained people I had met. I told Greg that he might have found the spiritual friend he'd been looking for. This fellow pilgrim had come to Greg, trusting him with issues he would not speak of elsewhere. This is a very good beginning for a peer-to-peer conversation about life.

Somewhere, there is a friend or friends that have the capacity to share your inner journey with you and God at a deep and ongoing level. Please note that this is not connecting, and then quickly disconnecting, because there is nothing in it for you. It is building friendships that last through all the uncertainties and turbulence that life brings. If we are not prepared to endure the tough times, we certainly will not have the privilege of sharing the good ones.

I have been guilty of some pretty bad starts in friendships. I have seen others with very good intentions step on the landmines of relationship that damage the potential for growth in spiritual friendship. Lofty goals, expectations of performance, impatience and demands for transparency and accountability are just a few of those landmines.

Friendships cannot grow in the spiritual dimension if we demand predetermined outcomes. The only expectation we must try to bring to the relationship is that God wants to join us in our conversations and invites us to know the presence of the Holy Spirit. True spiritual friendship surrenders control of the friendship to the Holy Spirit. It engages at the precise place we are currently at in our lives. It needs—first and foremost—to be about loving relationship, not accomplishment.

I have started some spiritual friendships with the intention to have a curriculum, a book list, a weekly meeting, and a list of weaknesses to shore up. Those ended on a dead-end street.

Friendships that connect with the Holy Spirit have to trust the Holy Spirit's work in each life in the friendship. True spiritual companions are peers, mutually committed to growing in the knowledge and experience of Jesus from revelation through scripture, creation, and most particularly, God's incarnate presence in each one.

Performance expectations get in the way of this freedom. We may have very different views of what makes a mature believer, what shapes a growing one, and what corrects the careless. Passion for becoming better, combined with compassion for our shared weaknesses, creates a healthy ground for a spiritual seed to grow and become fruitful.

Another performance expectation that can be very destructive is the desire that friendship will lead to some shared missional activity. Being together listening to God does not mean we will head out together to feed the hungry or whatever very righteous and worthy cause might be my passion. I spend a good portion of my time with friends helping with their discernment of what their call is from the Holy Spirit in decision-making, family conflict, vocational issues or social responsibility. It is never my job to give vision. Seldom is it my role to join in their mission.

Safety from these expectations is essential. It is in these safe environments that we may hear very different—while equally radical—calls from God on our life. The best spiritual companions endeavour to assist in authentic listening to God and support whatever changes may be required. But there is no expectation that the vision received for one will be the same for both.

My friend Ron and I pray together, but our missions are very different. We help each other discern what God may be saying during our times together, and the insight we receive is later expressed in our very different missional activities.

My conversations with many friends are not about developing a common mission, but about knowing how each of us is to best respond to the call of God and the needs of the world we see. Our personal mission statements may change, but our common desire to know and follow Christ is the constant. I am simply helping clear the path to Jesus' mind for another. It's a bit like John the Baptist. He said, "I am not the Messiah. I am here to prepare the way for him—that is all" (John 3:27–30 NRSV).

I remember hearing an old country preacher say, "You don't go out in the garden every day and pull up the carrots you've planted to see if they are growing, so why do we do this in the spiritual world? The carrots will be dead before they get to grow and some spirits get killed the same way." We often try to measure our spiritual lives the way we analyze our investments. What we are worth on paper changes many times a day. We are never sure when it is going to go up or down. But our value as friends of God is always high. It is our perception of ourselves that can grow darker than it ought. If we have honest friendships, we will not lie to one another about issues of failure or lack of self-awareness. We will remind one another that we are looked on by the God who loves us and sees our whole person—not just the dark thing we may be focusing on.

My friend Daryl and I met occasionally over the 25 years we have known each other, usually at his request, and usually at a time of transition in his life. We met to follow up on some things we had been working on together in a vocational transition. Our meetings opened him up to friendship in a new way. At our initial meeting over lunch, I explained my approach to friendship. If he invited me to be his companion I would agree, but it would have no agenda or expectation of outcome or return. Usually I simply say, "Let's develop our friendship and see where the Holy Spirit takes us."

Many years have passed. Daryl recently said that he finally believed me. I wasn't sure what he meant. He reminded me of my promise of a friendship without agenda. But he had not really believed that it was possible.

What sealed this spiritual friendship for me personally, was the moment I realized that we were equally vulnerable. Through his insights, Daryl forced me to face an insecurity he observed in me—anxiety that seemed out of proportion at an event at which I was to speak. I tried to pass it off as simple nerves. I told him that my nerves helped me keep my edge. He wasn't convinced. He had no idea how important that conversation was. It set the groundwork for a very important process that a few friends helped me through over the next few months. It was a very basic lesson in conversation with God. It focused on a key area of understanding for all of us when we are down on ourselves for poor performance, behaviour and embarrassment. During that time, a variety of conversations ensued with friends who noticed this same tendency in me. One good friend wrote a note to himself that said, quite bluntly: Norm's self-image is shit.

That very graphic metaphor about my inner life spurred me to explore this area with Tarcia, my spiritual director. I wanted to explore this issue in prayer. Tarcia encouraged me to ask myself these questions: Is this true? Is it a real failure, a moral issue? If it is true, then is it the total truth about my life? If it were, would my life be what it is today? And finally, am I speaking to myself about this issue the way Jesus would? If not, why not? I offered thanks for the reminder of my need for help. I confessed, made right the issue, and didn't let it further define me.

That little process has been a terrific way to transform inner turmoil into constructive conversation with God and a few close friends, over and over again. Instead of allowing persistent notes of condemnation or confusion to dominate, I found a way to deal constructively and openly with core issues, with God and a friend or two.

My experience with Daryl, and the path it led me on, is a perfect example of how we learn about spiritual formation through conversation with those who have the ability to listen well to our lives, but also have some wisdom in how to deal with things constructively and conversationally with God. Who could have expected such deep transformation stemming from a relationship built on a foundation that was actually free of expectations?

Being together with friends without expectation is a very hard discipline. We are trained to get something out of every experience. But if experience of the presence of each other is important, then anticipation of certain outcomes only becomes a distraction. This is where the connection with the old historic streams of faith is very instructive. Historic figures from ancient Church history, like Benedict of Nursia, Francis of Assisi, the Celtic monastics and Ignatius of Loyola to name a few, had a holy passion to be the best followers of Jesus they could be. They recognized that spiritual growth started with listening with our whole being to the revelation of God in Christ through scripture, creation and incarnation.

They all developed different missions like education, helping the poor and building the Church, yet they never compromised their commitment to listening to what was going on in their spiritual lives first. Nothing could replace their relationship with God. They lived a commitment to extended, undisturbed times of listening to God.

Extensive time listening is also the foundation for spiritual friendship. We can care and pray for one another, but we must be patient with the slowness of progress, or a complete lack of progress, as we might normally define it. Fruitful friendship is a slow growing fruit, but it lasts over many seasons.

Even though mutual transparency is a must-have in spiritual friendship, expecting it too soon can derail the relationship.

I have seen friends try being intentional about their spiritual friendship, assuming they will both immediately share the deepest sins they have recently committed. Once that expectation is set—that full disclosure is always required—the plant of friendship can quickly shrivel. Disclosure of that nature, at that level, can and should take time to develop naturally.

My friend Ron and I have been spending time being present to one another for over 30 years. We have high levels of transparency. But it is not forced. It is encouraged by years of trust, both in confidentiality and in non-judgemental response. Nothing hurts honesty more than forcing it. And crying, "You did what?!" kills it.

Some of my spiritual friends are leaders, writers, and pastors in our various faith streams. Others are the congregants, supporters and volunteers who hear their public communication. I hear from my leader, pastor, writer friends about the broken places in life, where they have most profoundly experienced the love and grace of God. They have doubts about some dogma in their constituency. They have moral failures and inner struggles. But a climate of judgement keeps them silent about these things, except in the safest of places.

Then, I hear the stories of the men and women who listen to these leaders. They believe their experience of life and God to be very different from that of their leaders. They believe the leaders have it all together. They know there is grace in Christ for their broken spaces, but find such grace mostly in conversations with trusted friends, small groups and on retreats, just like their leaders do.

It is as though we have two concentric circles of faith experience, hermetically sealed from one another, and unable to connect at the soul level for health and healing or true community building. Neither group is dishonest, but the religious structures within which we operate make it extremely difficult for our leaders to speak with candour about how confusing and grey life really can be. Friendship that connects at the emotional-spiritual level is almost an act of civil disobedience. We hear the voice of Christ that says to follow him. And that he loves us unconditionally.

I saw a fresco in a cathedral in Florence called "The Trinity" painted by Masaccio in the 1400s. It is a stunning depiction of Jesus on the cross, 25 feet high. The Father is right behind him with arms extended supporting the cross. The Holy Spirit is in the form of a dove at Jesus' head. Father, Son and Spirit are pictured together at the cross. I looked for a long time at this image, imagining with the artist that when Jesus shouted, "My God, my God why have you forsaken me?" the Father was right there, holding him up in his greatest moment of darkness. In his greatest moments of desolation and abandonment, his groans and inarticulate cries were being expressed by the Spirit.

In the same way, we are never alone. No matter how desperate the circumstances, no matter how deep our fear, whatever our cross, the Loving Three are always with us. Below the cross in the fresco is an open tomb with a body being brought back to life. It represents all of humanity. Engraved on that tomb are the words, "I was that which you are. You will be that which I am."

That is the point of spiritual friendship: to be in relationship with Jesus in such a way that his incarnational presence in life, and now personally in our lives, transforms us quietly and progressively into conformity with his character. It is not about knowing doctrine in our heads, it is knowing Jesus in the deepest places of our whole being—body, mind, soul and spirit.

It is risky to embark on a spiritual journey as mutual learners rather than experts. But, the strongest place to be of help to another is as a learner. Knowledge of how much you don't know is a good place to be even though it is, of course, more an attitude than a reality. When we are learners, there is no danger of one of us needing control or the right answers. We are on an adventure of discovery of what the Holy Spirit is doing in us.

We underestimate what we already know about life and God. It is surprising to us that another person may value our wisdom when we certainly don't see ourselves as wise. We've become so specialized in our culture that we too frequently think only of the professionals (counselors, pastors, spiritual directors), when a friend shares a need or problem. Often, when a friend asks me to act as the professional with someone else, I'll suggest that they respond to the need themselves. More often than not, they have wisdom and experience that is helpful for their friend. They just lack the confidence and permission to act.

A banker's experience with God, offered to an investment analyst, is received with greater power than any words I can offer. It is the wisdom of peers that has the most power, those who know the reality of our particular world. I have experience and wisdom, but when a person has experienced loss they need one who has also experienced their type of pain to authentically offer comfort and perspective. Little in our professionalized culture encourages us to listen deeply to God at work in our own lives. Yet, what I hear in the lives of others, strikes me as gold—experience ready to be mined for wisdom. We move together into uncharted territory of trusting that God is present in our being together, and wanting to join us in relationship. Listening deeply to each other—without needing to offer advice—creates a context of discovery that leads to true divine wisdom.

During Touchstone retreats we offer plenty of time and space for private reflection on the life of Jesus and his love for us. The real joy often comes when we gather after our silent reflections to share with the group what we have experienced. Often, more is learned about the experience by the teller than the listeners as they share their experience. Emotions, discoveries, and joyful wisdom become clear because of the generosity of the listeners. We learn much when we share with trusted friends the things that are actually happening in our lives.

It is in the safety, sanctity and mystery of friendship where we frequently share our insecurity about having anything of value to offer. This is when growth happens. Time after time, I have witnessed deep and often startling moments of discovery in Touchstone groups. I may offer thoughts to help or encourage, but frequently the most powerful connection is made between the "non-professional" members of the group.

Because our culture is so afraid of pain and suffering and focused on success and performance, it is hard to keep spiritual journey in perspective. The danger is that we become so focused on our own needs and problems that we fail to focus on the Divine Shepherd whose death on the cross shows us the path of true life and humanity.

Engaging with a friend on spiritual friendship's path is not a narcissistic search for escape. Rather, spiritual friendship takes us—together—down whatever road of joy and sorrow comes our way. We discover the love of God in the company of another learning the downward path to lifting up our souls and lives.

CHAPTER 6

ANCIENT TRADITIONS AND SPIRITUAL FRIENDSHIP

We live in what is called Headwaters Country, just north of Toronto. Our community is at the source of several rivers, some running north and some south. All supply water to millions of people for consumption, recreation, manufacturing, bathing and all the many life-giving uses that water has.

A child jumping into a lake 75 miles from here, and exulting in her splashing, is not conscious of all the springs, streams and rivers that created her experience. That is like the experience many of us have with faith in Jesus. Just like the many streams that feed our lakes and rivers, and many unseen underground streams that feed the river, there is a diversity of ancient streams that have fed our various traditions of faith formation. Tapping into those today can help nurture our spiritual friendships.

Susan and I were in Italy for a conference to study the Renaissance. We travelled to Assisi to explore the life of St. Francis. It was a powerful experience for us all to be immersed in his life and work. A friend on the trip said that she felt sad that, as a Presbyterian, Francis was not part of her heritage. I begged to differ. Because Francis' life predates the Reformation and the schism that ensued, Francis is very much part of our heritage. Our friend found that comforting. We have a much broader set of resources in our history as followers of Jesus than we may be aware of.

There is a direct connection between the practices preserved in some of the monastic traditions to this day, and the quest for becoming better listeners to God, our own lives and the lives of spiritual friends.

As I journeyed out of the richness of my evangelical heritage, with its passion for truth and mission, I also longed for ways to more deeply digest the faith that I outwardly expressed. I longed for growth. My particular faith heritage limited my scope. I needed more.

When I first read authors like Jean Vanier, Richard Foster and Eugene Peterson, I heard a hint of the springs running under the surface of my religious superstructure. Many people were talking about forms of prayer that I had never heard of. I was like a person flying a jet who had read the instruction manual, but had not actually flown under the guidance and training of an expert pilot. You can get into some amazing crashes with only theoretical knowledge at your disposal.

The really expert pilot is the Holy Spirit. Our honest desire to point ourselves toward God places us in safe territory, no matter how crude our understanding. Listening, rather than talking, seems to be the beginning point. I was raised to proclaim my faith in word, and at the same time, to bring requests and confessions to God. As I grew older, that type of prayer seemed more mechanical than relational.

My friend Jack and I partnered doing retreats with men for a few years. We sent them away for extended times of silent reflection on scripture. We discovered a power in that silent reflection that allowed for personal discovery. Then, when the men shared later in a group what they had learned, there were compelling lessons for the rest of the group to hear about. Jack and I learned that our level of internal and external distraction can be almost overwhelming. We also discovered that once a group has taken time to listen deeply to God, it creates a very different atmosphere for communication. Rather than listening to a speaker or discussing or even debating a text, we were coming to listen to the life of another person. We could see and hear what Jesus would reveal of himself in that person's discoveries.

Most of us are very good at being verbal. And most of us are not very good at listening to our own lives. Silence creates the space for this kind of listening, but travelling in strange territory sometimes requires a map. Unaccustomed as I may be to asking directions, that is ultimately what I did.

There is a bit of mystical and mythical chatter around the term *spiritual direction.* It means nothing other than asking for directions in unfamiliar areas of your life. Spiritual direction is not about escaping into some special, safe place where life is always good. It is about travelling paths that may seem intimidating. With help, we discover that the light of Jesus shines best in even the darkest places.

I was finally ready to ask direction and find this funny type of person called a spiritual director. I had done extensive reading about the subject and now I was on a quest to try it on for size. Tarcia, a spiritual director trained and experienced in the wisdom of Ignatius became my spiritual companion.

Thomas Merton describes the role of a spiritual director as "God's usher" enabling another to hear an authentic word from God themselves, not telling them what they ought to think.

Tarcia's gentle and focused guidance led me through an experience of Ignatius' training program. I discovered a door to imaginative and liberating listening to God and the Holy Spirit's moving in my life. What I was moving toward was not leading me away from the foundational faith of my Baptist heritage. My background gave me a strong grounding in the scriptures, and a passion to know and serve Christ. The new things I am learning take me more profoundly into the very soil from which my faith sprouted. The Ignatian tradition is strongly shaped by scripture, but encourages the use of all our senses to experience it. The contemplative traditions help us add an experience of heart, soul and mind to our intellectual faith.

Tarcia slowly led me into listening prayer by saying, "I want to teach you the prayer of faith." It was a prayer that felt passive. It was not the active prayer of seeing mountains fall into the sea. Tarcia asked me to believe that, as I sit in silence, perhaps not even reflecting on scripture, God is present and wanting to communicate with me.

This is a real beginning point for friendship with God and those in our life. Sitting quietly, without agenda, and waiting expectantly to see what may happen in the quiet, is a discipline that leads to creative freedom. The more comfortable we are with quietly listening to God, the better we will listen to our friends.

Ignatius taught his followers to be imitators of the life of Jesus. He believed that knowing Jesus' story, with all our being, would lead us to imitate his life. So Ignatius developed the idea of praying a story from Jesus' life.

A few years ago I read an interview with Irish actor Liam Neeson in a national newspaper. He discussed an eye-opening discovery he had about the spiritual roots of his acting craft when he was shooting *The Mission*, a movie that told the story of a Jesuit mission in South America. Jesuit priest Daniel Berrigan was an advisor for the movie and the two of them chatted during shooting breaks. Berrigan asked Neeson if he knew that his method acting approach—of becoming the character he was portraying—had spiritual roots. Surprised, Neeson commented that acting was far from spiritual. He just got painted up and said some lines, and then moved on to things that mattered more. But Berrigan explained that the creator of method acting developed it by copying the *Spiritual Exercises* of Ignatius. Ignatius encourages us to take a brief story from the Gospels, and by spending extended time in silence and letting our imaginations take us into the story, we connect with Jesus in a profound way.

Just as an actor becomes a character he portrays, so we become actors in the life of Jesus, and then become more connected to his life and ministry. As we become more connected to Jesus' life, we become more aware of the competition in our own souls for attention and satisfaction.

It is fascinating to me that the writer of Hebrews has a similar idea about really connecting with those for whom we pray. After encouraging us all to mutual love and hospitality for strangers he adds, "Remember those who are in prison, *as though you were in prison with them*; those who are being tortured, *as though you yourselves were being tortured*" (Hebrews 13:3 NRSV). Imagining myself in prison or being tortured is a remarkable act of the imagination, but creative use of our imaginations is a valuable gift God gives us for connecting with him and each other.

There are a number of prayer forms that have been preserved in religious orders that today remain within the Roman Catholic Church. But they have been preserved for the whole Church, and are actually a gift to the whole Church. They are not owned by one particular tradition.

The traditional terms to describe them are *Lectio Divina*, "Praying the Memories of Jesus," *Collatio*, "Centering Prayer" and "Imitative Prayer." When I use these prayers on my own, with a friend or in a group, I remove the traditional terms and describe them as "listening to God with a friend or friends," or "listening to God," or "imagining yourself in a story from Jesus' life."

I change the names to allow us to more easily experience these traditional tools, without worrying about it being some weird or onerous task. Collatio, at first hearing, sounds like I'm clearing my throat. Depending on our tradition we can be suspicious of practices that are unfamiliar. Latin names only add to this suspicion. These forms of praying require effort and discipline on our part, but we joyfully and gratefully learn to receive from the God who comes to us.

We are trying to escape the noise of life, and listen to what is going on beneath the surface. We share a desire to make our journey with Jesus more real and part of all of our life. We know how hard it is to find time and space to do any of this with regularity. The listening prayer methods combine the security of scripture's story, relational connection and deep reflection that can lead to transformation of who we are on a daily basis.

Listening prayer also leads to connectedness with other people's stories, as we connect with the story of Jesus. It is here that transformation in relationships can occur. When we spend time with a friend or a small group, and commit to avoiding distractions and focusing on God in creation, scripture and relationships, we are changed. We move from being frenetic competitors to more gentle and aware listeners.

Travelling the prayer road with Jesus in ways that connect him with his life on earth—and connect us with his ongoing work in the world in which we live—happens slowly. I am going to offer some suggestions on how to put prayer into practice with a friend or in a group. There is no right or wrong way to do anything that is about pointing your life intentionally in God's direction. If you have this desire, you are already in a good place. Your longing is evidence that the God who loves you is at work, to give you not only the interest in pursuing spiritual friendships, but the strength and ability.

The strongest position from which to teach others is as a learner. I invite you to learn along with me, and you invite me along to learn with and from you. We are connected by a mutual desire to grow in friendship with God and with each other. We are not in charge of the process or the life of the other. We mutually submit to the Holy Spirit. Jesus said it blows like the breeze (John 3:8). You may be surprised when and how it gusts. And so we climb into the sailboat of spiritual voyage and see where the Holy Spirit blows us.

For control and outcome types like most of us, this is a wonderful exercise in being pioneers and adventurers. We don't know where it will lead us, or what joys and dangers may lie ahead. But we know we go in companionship with Jesus and each other.

CHAPTER 7

A RETREAT WITH A SPIRITUAL FRIEND

I don't want to bore you with prescriptions and directions for doing a retreat with a friend. Instead, let me tell you about a recent retreat I did with my friend Ron. You will see that our retreat was intentionally unintentional—and yet placed us in a space that enriched our relationship with God and each other.

Learn from our process by imitation and rejection.

Ron's flight arrived in Toronto and he emerged from the terminal around 9:45 a.m. on a sunny June morning. He tossed his luggage into my car and we headed up the highway to embark on a retreat together for the umpteenth time in our long friendship. The car was turned north. Our minds were turned toward God. Our intentions were directed to deepening our friendship. But there was nothing "religious" about our behaviour. We looked like any two geezers drinking our Tim Horton's coffee as we drove.

Ray Simpson, a mentor and guide in the Celtic tradition, wrote this friendship prayer:

> Gentle God, reveal to us the beauty of sensitive friendship.
> Help us to create such stillness in our inner being
> that we become aware of your gracious movements
> in the souls of others.[1]

That's the goal Ron and I have when we embark on our semi-annual retreats. God engages us where we are—not where we wish we were—so the journey to friendship with God at the centre may look very unreligious. If you are at all like us, busy, aggressive, goal-oriented and with many responsibilities, sensitive friendship and inner stillness seem far on the horizon. But that is the goal of our journey when we do a retreat together.

The two hour drive to a friend's cottage was spent chatting about anything top of mind: the latest political news, family updates, and work and health challenges: the top of the surface of our lives. Unpacking groceries and bedding, and settling into the cottage took us a bit of time. Then we headed into nearby Parry Sound for lunch. The restaurant has a porch overlooking the harbour and it was a great place to watch boats and aircraft in the harbour.

More conversation over our beer and fish and chips continued, but the questions we asked one another started to become more focused. Our willingness to really listen to the answers was key to leaving our daily grind behind and becoming truly present to one another. A seaplane was rumbling to takeoff so we ambled down for a better look. Grabbing an ice cream cone we sat on a bench looking out at the water.

---

1.   Cited from Ray Simpson, ed. *Celtic Prayers for Life Today,* No. 292, p. 292.

We shared silence, but also a clear focus on what was currently giving hope to our lives and what different issues were confusing or weighing on us. It was a shared desire to hear and understand what was going on under the surface of our lives—beyond the latest gossip, political controversy or media scandal.

The rest of the day we walked, sat on the dock, prepared dinner, listened to music, and enjoyed a fine meal, some wine and a glass of port. All this was getting us settled in each other's presence and preparing us for a day of conscious listening to God the next morning.

The very mundane quality of our day is important. Ron and I both know that we can't hurry friendship. Under most circumstances the pace of the day would have driven us nuts. There was no task other than getting relaxed together, conscious that God was present even as we smoked an evening cigar and chatted about life.

Getting settled enough to truly listen to life—mine and a friend's—requires the disciplines of simplicity and quiet. We share a mutual trust that God exists and communicates in the silence. Equally important, we are confident that the other has our best interests at heart. If you want to deepen a spiritual friendship, you may have to relax and let the Holy Spirit guide you in the holy mundane. It's about settling down.

We are both early risers, so next morning we sat with our coffee after breakfast in the screened-in porch. We watched the rain pour and the mist cloud the lake. But our vision was clear. We opened our Bibles and read Psalm 139 out loud to each other twice. We took turns reading. Then, we sat in the silence to listen to what we may have heard from our gracious God. In our private and shared prayers we sometimes use the following ancient prayer form:

A SIMPLE WAY TO PRAY A PASSAGE OF SCRIPTURE

Take time to hear a passage of scripture uncritically and non-analytically. There is no other goal than becoming passive and receptive in the presence of the sound of the words. As we hear ourselves reading the words aloud, we listen for "a word from God."

That word or phrase that catches our attention becomes the word on which we will take time to meditate. We believe that God is speaking to us through it. The word we leave this exercise with is a gift for the day to take with us. We are reminded by that word of the presence of God in our lives.

This is a kind of attentive reading and listening prayer that spiritual friends can do together.

Read aloud: Read a passage several times and listen to the Word of God. Listen for a special "word" from God in the passage. What word or phrase catches your attention?

Meditate: Ponder, reflect, and let your mind roam freely over the word you have been given. Don't analyze. Just see where the word takes you in thoughts about God and your life.

Speak: Talk to God in prayer with thoughts and responses to the word. Have a good chat with God about whatever is on your mind at this time.

Reflect: Taste the word. Sit still in the presence of God. Is there a thought or feeling you have at the end of this experience? Share these with your friend.

After a period of silence, Ron and I chatted about what we heard from God as we listened together. This can be a remarkable experience, simple and relatively easy to do. There are no right or wrong answers or interpretations. There is no competition or argument. Congenial togetherness is fostered. We are conscious of hearing God speak through scripture, the creation around us and the incarnational presence of Jesus in one another. On many occasions the words or phrases that caught our attention in that 30-minute conversation shape or guide our conversations for the rest of the day.

Being geezers, we need a refill on our coffees at some point. We settled back in to the presence of God by listening to a story from the Gospels. This time our prayer was called "Imitative Prayer," or the theme that admiration leads to transformation.

IMITATIVE PRAYER

Remember Paul's words to the Philippians:

"Finally, beloved, whatever is true, whatever is honorable, whatever is just, whatever is pure, whatever is pleasing, whatever is commendable, if there is any excellence and if there is anything worthy of praise, think about these things" (Philippians 4:8 NRSV). In the past, I've heard these words as a burden, rather than a simple encouragement for a better vision that nurtures my true humanity at its best. Sometimes, when we use words like "contemplative," or "centering," to describe prayer we can focus more on technique than on the organic, loving experience of God.

St. Francis' influential prayer companion was a woman named Clare. Her passion to know Jesus deeply led her to what she called Imitative Prayer. Clare focused her imitative longing particularly on the crucifixion stories of Jesus. The mystery and accessibility of God in Jesus captured her, particularly his humility in his arrest, trial and execution. Clare's prayer pattern takes the following simple but challenging form:

Gaze: What do you see, hear, experience? Quietly and undistracted, look at the One you love.

Consider: The character and love of God in Jesus Christ. How are you drawn to his ways? What do you notice about Jesus in this story?

Contemplate: Where does the Jesus of this story connect with your life now? How are you challenged and encouraged by his humble and sacrificial love?

Imitate: "We become what we love and who we love shapes what we become."[2] Let what you have seen shape who you become.

From our earliest moments, we learn our way of living by imitating others. As kids, we watch and imitate our parents, then peers and our elders as we mature. The models we choose to imitate shape the trajectory of our life. The same is true when we read scripture and pray. True prayer draws us deep into the loving heart of God to bring hope, health and healing. It is not another task to complete, a set of rules to obey or an elitist route to a stress-free life.

In admiring the life of Jesus in a Gospel story, we connect with his life. His life connects with our own. As we are drawn to his ways we reflect on our lives. Where do we notice the presence of Jesus in the brokenness of the world we serve?

---

2. Illia Delio, *Franciscan Prayer.* Cincinnati, Ohio: St. Anthony Messenger Press, 2004.

Greater awareness of the life of Jesus in us leads us to a greater sensitivity to notice his presence in others.

Jesus is the highest expression of what it means to be most truly human. Imitative prayer is a quiet and reflective way to a relationship with Jesus at his most humble and yet most trans-forming. Imitative prayer is a subtle but powerful variation on contemplative prayer. Clare believed that our prayers ought first to focus on Gospel stories, particularly the stories around the cross. We gaze on the humble and vulnerable Redeemer as he goes through his final humiliation. Our admiration for Jesus' powerful love and sacrifice affects us deeply. We will want to imitate it. We become what we admire. And we want to become like Jesus in his life and death.

As we internalize our admiration of Jesus' life and work we may look back on a day or week and notice subtle changes in our own life and work. Keep your eyes open to see this. Irenaeus, an early Church father, is quoted as saying: "The glory of God is the human being fully alive and the life of the human consists in beholding God." We use imitative prayer to scrape beneath the crusty surface of our lives that accumulates and hardens, inevitably and inexorably. We find hope, comfort, truth, pain, the grit of life, the scars along with the holy presence of God who chooses to incarnate his life and love in our skin and bone.

Jesus, by the Spirit, resides in even the darkest places of our lives assuring us of love, forgiveness and redemption. We discover hope and reality in the mystery of the Divine Presence in all of life. We see Jesus' presence in our daily lives when we have gazed with wonder and love on his love and humility—his birth, life of love, redemptive death and powerful resurrection. To his glory, Jesus not only shows us, but empowers us, to be fully human.

In the spirit of this prayer form, Ron and I read Luke's story of Jesus' trip to the cross. We began when Simon takes the cross from Jesus. We read to his last words and death. Reading it out loud—twice—allowed us to use our senses to receive the story. It was set in our imaginative mind's eye.

For the next 90 minutes we stayed in silence, reflecting and gazing. We let our eyes and imaginations take in the story – trusting the Holy Spirit to guide our thoughts. On this occasion we used Clare's prayer pattern but we have frequently used the following pattern created by Ignatius:

USE YOUR IMAGINATION TO PRAY A STORY FROM JESUS' LIFE

1. Select a brief action passage of scripture.
2. Relax and settle into God's presence.
3. Slowly read the passage aloud. Allow the scene to sink into your imagination.
4. Slowly read the passage a second time, looking for details you missed the first time. Look away from the page. Let the scene unfold in your imagination.
5. Slowly read it a third time. You will notice more details. Questions, interpretations and insights will occur to you. Let them settle in your memory for 30 seconds. We are too accustomed to embracing these questions and interpretations, but they distract us from becoming part of the story.
6. Read a fourth or even fifth time, until these distractions quiet. Put the Bible aside.
7. Let the scene happen in your mind. Sink into the scene. Eventually you will become part of it.

8. Interact with the characters in the scene. Help them with their work. Listen to their conversations and reply to their questions and comments.

9. Don't moralize or make applications. You will find application naturally, as you reflect.

10. When the prayer period ends, review what happened with your spiritual friend. Did you notice tension, confusion, encouragement or challenge? The tension may be something you need to return to for further prayer. Give thanks to God for being present with you during this time of prayer.

When the 90 minutes were up, Ron and I settled into comfortable chairs, lit a cigar and sat in quiet for a few minutes. For the next hour we quietly discussed the struggle of becoming quiet, the part of the story that captured our attention and then the experience we had.

Ron had ended up becoming the cross-carrier and I had spent time with the gamblers at the foot of the cross. Both of us had had very distinct experiences of the presence of God, and yet were drawn together in our differences.

If it hadn't been pouring rain, we would have gone for a walk or a kayak ride, something to break the intensity. Instead, we went for lunch and found ourselves continuing to explore the prayer experience of the morning. Our conversation focused on how the life and death of Jesus, as we experienced it that morning, connected to our struggle to adjust to our changing lives.

The afternoon was a time of relaxation. Our body rhythms want quiet space and even a nap before we engage in further discussion. By 5:00 p.m. we returned to our view of the lake and renewed conversation. We shared questions about what we had expressed earlier, but offered no advice. As we have opportunity to ask honest questions, we find wisdom and clarity as we answer. Light dinner, quiet conversation and a glass of port ended the day.

The final morning we packed up and headed back to the airport. But before we did, we had space for God in our friendship. Coffee in hand, we read another Gospel story out loud and sat in the silence, listening. The conversation gathered some loose threads from the day before. The table was set for our conversation as we drove to the airport. We were quiet, grateful for God's love and each other. We had laid foundation for future discoveries.

There is nothing magical about having a retreat like this with a friend. But there is some mystery when you intentionally spend time together for several hours with no agenda but friendship with God and each other. It is also wonderfully safe. We discuss many confidential subjects in our lives like marriage, family, money, sex and power – the normal gamut of issues we face. Our lives continue in our selected vocations and geographies. But our connection with one another remains deep and strong.

We are two friends who want a friendship with Jesus. We know that we help one another toward that friendship with our own.

CHAPTER 8

NOW WHAT?

"So what to do, now that I've read this book?" Good question. It may be that some of my ideas seem too far ahead of where you are right now—or else too shallow! There are 30 years of intentional actions on my part behind this work, and 30 years of mistakes and wrong turns. You and your friends may be cut from very different cloth—but there are some core lessons about spiritual friendship that can help any friendship, at any stage.

Intentionality, time, space, silence, listening to your own life and the life of another. Listening to God and commitment even in conflict. Those are a few key things I would encourage you to explore when you are considering spiritual friendship. Remember, a spiritual friendship is not a mechanical exercise, but is life and health giving in a way that is unique and profound.

John the Baptist is a helpful prototype. When asked if the emerging ministry of Jesus was competition to his own work, he spoke these creative, passionate and even unlikely words for a camel hair-shirted, insect-eating prophet: "God in heaven appoints each person's work. You yourselves know how plainly I told you that I am not the Messiah. I am here to prepare the way for him—that is all. The bride will go where the bridegroom is. A bridegroom's friend rejoices with him. I am the bridegroom's friend, and I am filled with joy at his success. He must become greater and greater, and I must become less and less"(John 3:27–30 NLT).

John has a strong sense of who he is. He is joyful in his role in life as the one who prepares the way for Jesus' ministry to be launched. John rejoices in the success of Jesus' mission to the extent that even his own disciples were free to leave and form the core of Jesus' disciple group.

True spiritual friendship has that kind of intentionality at its core. Spiritual friendship prepares the way for another to find relationship with God in Christ. Strong individual identities unite toward the goal of the other being successful—whatever success may mean to each one. Spiritual friendship makes room for the other in a way that inspires growth and freedom—without expectation of return.

Remember though, John also had self-doubts. As he languished in Herod's prison awaiting execution he sent friends to Jesus asking if he was really The One John thought he was. We are more like John than we realize. Often, our strong core identities are rattled by the realities of life. We wonder about choices we've made, and if we can find a fresh start when we have a lifetime of accumulated obligations and responsibilities.

Any spiritual friendship will have both sides of John's coin in its purse. One moment, we know we are the beloved children of God. The next moment, we are insecure persons desperately needing the affirmation of others. We want to prepare the way for someone else, but competing with this desire is our own need for attention and affirmation.

Relax in the process of discovery. Opening ourselves to God and to someone else is an act of faith. The outcome is unknown, yet the journey is worth it. As you find another friend to journey with you, set your expectations low, but be highly intentional about listening to God and each other.

Spiritual friendships do not need to be complicated. Whatever helps you listen to God, whatever helps you listen to the other—do those things.

Time and space are two very key ingredients for this process to develop. We are dealing with two types of time. One is the intentional time we spend together. In this particular time, we are listening to God in creation, scripture and and each other's stories. We invest significant time for building our connection with each other, in the pursuit of spiritual friendship.

The second sort of time is lifetime—the extended period over which we participate in the ebb and flow of life's experiences and develop our shared history. My first experiments in spiritual friendship began when I was early in marriage, children and career. Friendships that began then, now have the shared history of all the stages that followed, with their joys and sorrows, successes and failures. Friendship that grows through the many stages of life creates a maturity that can only come with age and experience. The good news is, those friendships can begin at any stage.

I've learned with my friends that the normal stages of life are God's gifts to us to expand our capacity to grow from self-centred people to those who can love widely and inclusively. The ways in which we embrace these normal stages of growth shape how mature and loving we become. Friendship grows and deepens as we move through these stages.

As these two sorts of time pass, a third sort of time emerges: *Kairos*. *Kairos* is different from the kind of time that dominates our culture; this is leisurely time, in which we experience one another and whatever situation we share. It is not measurable. It is experiential.

In the course of spending time together, spiritual friends nurture a mutual passivity and receptivity to the Holy Spirit's activity through listening to scripture, creation and each other. As you spend time sitting back and focusing on being present and hospitable to God and one another, you will find your conversation takes on a different kind of shape and depth.

Over time, you will be increasingly comfortable with shared silence. You will not feel compelled to fill in the gaps with words. A growing faith that God is present and communicating with us in the silence helps us welcome this growth. There is less need for filling silence when we believe it is already full of the presence of God. We grow in our ability to create space for one another through silence. Long gaps between statements allow for reflection, and discipline us against our propensity to express the first thought that enters our heads. It is amazing how much we learn about one another when there is plenty of space for conversation to shape itself—without hasty intrusion.

When we recognize the incarnational presence of Jesus in one another, we develop a deeper respect for silence. It is only in the silence that we can see, hear and experience Jesus in the other.

Time, space and patience, lived out over the long haul, are central to spiritual friendships. At the core is your own journey with Jesus and how you nurture it over time. Silent reflection—

employing whatever prayer tools are appropriate for you—is the doorway for your relationship with Jesus and a heightened awareness of what the Holy Spirit may be doing in your life. As you notice periods of joy, frustration, correction, failure, and maybe even depression, you find solace in prayer. It is noticing these rhythms in your own life that sensitizes your awareness of the same rhythms in a friend. The issues may be different for your friend, but the process is similar.

We bring to spiritual friendship a mutual journey of listening, discovery, change and correction. If one friend is not on the listening path, then there is really nothing to share. If only one half of the friendship is becoming sensitive to listening, the result is an imbalance.

We don't have homework to prepare for a conversation or retreat, but we bear a responsibility for our own growth to have something to offer another in sensitivity and care. It is also important for our own health that we have someone who will listen to our journey to keep us from becoming self-obsessed or even depressed in our reflections.

This same intimacy of relationship that provides support, care and love, can also open us to being wounded. The careless word, insensitive comment, or angry outburst of a friend can wound deeply. I have been the author—and the receiver—of what I jokingly refer to as an opportunity for character development.

True friendship among strong people will create tension that can lead to conflict. A friendship worth keeping is worth the effort it takes to resolve conflict in a healthy way. Once we realize that life is hard, we can accept that friendship is also hard. Friendship grows deepest when it is tested by conflict. My deepest wounds and my greatest acts of hurt have been with those I love. No relationship that is worth saving has been untested by fire.

The relationships that endure require forgiveness, patience and reconciliation in order to grow. My late mother once heard her friend say, "My Fred and I have not had a disagreement in the 50 years we have been married." "Then one of you has been doing all the thinking," said my mother. That's true of friendship: strong people with strong ideas will test and challenge one another. On occasion, misunderstanding or impatience will lead to conflict.

There is great joy in looking back at wounds healed and celebration over the restoration of relationship.

It is inevitable in life that we will face setbacks in marriage, family, finances, health and vocation, any area of life. If our friendship is only strong when times are easy, it isn't much of a friendship. I often say that if you want to know who my church is, see who showed up at my dad's funeral.

In the same way, friends show up in the times when we are embarrassed, rejected, excluded, and feel like a failure. Conflict explored and resolved prepares a friendship for other tough times.

This grittiness in friendship means that all subjects are fair game for exploration, or none are. Money, sex, power, dreams, fears, hopes, secret addictions and any other broken places are fair game for friends to explore, but only when it is mutually safe and comfortable. This is why the long game is important to remember; rushing into a false or forced transparency can kill the trust of a spiritual friendship. Search for ways to bring items that are of concern for you to the discussion but without judgement or preconception. If you or your friend are not ready to discuss a sensitive subject, then honour that sensitivity.

Creating safe space for another person to explore a broken place, a fear, or a concern is only accomplished with patience and mutual respect. For true spiritual friendship to grow candid at the core of life, we need to be on a journey of love, mercy, justice and patience ourselves. We enable one another to hear the voice of Jesus, the voice that says "come to me with your heavy burdens and learn from me" (Matthew 11:28–29).

We are not scrutinizing one another's weaknesses. It is easy to find another's faults. Discovering ways to come alongside and be a friend is completely the opposite. Spiritual friendship has a counter-cultural element. We look for truth combined with love and mercy. It is not prescriptive, authoritarian or scorekeeping.

Finding the heart and hearing the voice of Jesus is the real goal of spiritual friendship.

Reminding one another that Jesus speaks a word of love to the Father on our behalf, freeing us to change, grow and heal— and that Jesus also speaks to us—is also at the heart of spiritual friendship.

God knows your need of companionship. God will lead you in the appropriate time to those you are to engage on this adventure. Spiritual friendship is about finding one or two others who are longing for some quiet in the midst of the noise, and the opportunity to step back from the busyness of life to reflect. These companions are around you now and may just be waiting to see your interest in offering this gift to one another.

God knows your heart's desire is to love and serve Him. He knows it is not good to be alone in the journey. He has placed friends in your path. It may only take a small change to lead you together down this path of friendship that keeps awareness of God at its centre.

RECOMMENDED READING

*Books that have influenced my thinking
about spiritual friendship.*

Barry, William A. & Connolly, William J. *The Practice of Spiritual Direction*. New York: Seabury Press, 1982.

Bonhoeffer, Dietrich. *Meditating On The Word*. Cambridge, Mass.: Cowley, 1986.

Buechner, Frederick. *The Longing for Home*. San Francisco: HarperSanFrancisco,1996.

Campbell, Will D. *Brother to a Dragonfly*. New York: Seabury Press, 1977.

Chesterton, G.K. *The Everlasting Man*. Garden City, N.Y.: Image, 1985.

Chesterton, G.K. *Orthodoxy*. Dover Publications, 2004.

Delio, Ilia. *Franciscan Prayer*. Cincinnati, Ohio: St. Anthony Messenger Press, 2004.

Delio, Ilia. *The Humility of God* Cincinnati, Ohio: St. Anthony Messenger Press, 2005.

De Waal, Esther. *The Celtic Way of Prayer.* New York: Doubleday, 1997.

Dunne, Tad. *Spiritual Mentoring: Guiding People Through Spiritual Exercises to Life Decisions.* San Francisco: HarperSanFrancisco, 1991.

Eliot, T. S. *Selected Poems.* London: Faber, 1961.

Eliot, T. S. *Four Quartets.* London: Faber, 1964.

Ellul, Jacques. *The Politics of God & the Politics of Man.* Grand Rapids: Eerdmans, 1972.

Ellul, Jacques. *The Humiliation of the Word.* Grand Rapids: Eerdmans, 1985.

Foster, Richard J. *Celebration of Discipline.* San Francisco: Harper & Row, 1988.

Greeley, Andrew M. *May the Wind Be at Your Back.* New York: Seabury Press, 1975.

Heschel, Abraham Joshua. *The Sabbath.* Toronto: Harper Collins Canada, 1995.

Kierkegaard, Søren. *Gospel of Sufferings.* London: J. Clarke, 1982.

Lewis, C. S. *Prayer: Letters to Malcolm.* London: Fontana Books, 1974.

Green, Julien. *God's Fool: The Life & Times of Francis of Assisi.* San Francisco: Harper & Row, 1985.

Green, S. J Thomas H. *Drinking From a Dry Well.* Notre Dame: Ave Maria Press, 1991.

MacDonald, George. *Getting to Know Jesus.* New Canaan, Conn.: Keats Publishing, 1980.

MacDonald, George. *Proving the Unseen.* New Canann, Conn.: Keats Publishing, 1989.

Marty, Martin E. *Friendship.* Allen, Tex.: Argus Communications, 1980.

Merton, Thomas. *Spiritual Direction and Meditation & What is Contemplation?* Wheathampstead: A. Clarke, 1975.

Moran, Bob. *A Closer Look at Catholicism: a Guide for Protestants.* Waco, Tex.: Word Books, 1986.

Newbigin, Leslie. *The Gospel in a Pluralist Society.* Grand Rapids: W. B. Eerdmans, 1989.

Newell, J. Philip. *Celtic Prayers from Iona.* New York: Paulist Press, 1997.

O'Connor, Elizabeth. *Journey Inward, Journey Outward.* New York: Harper & Row, 1975.

O'Donohue, John. *Anam Cara.* New York: Harper Collins, 1997.

Oliva, Max. *The Masculine Spirit.* Notre Dame: Ave Maria Press, 1997.

Payne, Leanne. *The Broken Image.* Grand Rapids: Baker Publishing Group, 1996.

Peck, M. Scott. *The Different Drum: Community Making and Peace.* New York: Simon & Schuster, 1987.

Pennington, Basil M. *Lectio Divina: Renewing the Ancient Practice of Praying the Scriptures.* New York: Crossroad Publishing, 1998.

Phillips, J. B. *Ring of Truth.* London: Hodder & Stoughton, 1967.

Rolheiser, Ronald. *The Restless Heart: Finding our Spiritual Home.* New York: Doubleday, 2004.

Rolheiser, Ronald. *The Holy Longing: the Search for a Christian Spirituality.* New York: Doubleday, 1999.

Ryan, John K. *The Confessions of St. Augustine.* New York: Image Books, 1960.

Silf, Margaret. *Inner Compass: an Invitation to Ignatian Spirituality.* Chicago, Ill.: Loyola Press, 1999.

Simpson, Ray. *Celtic Blessings: Prayers for Everyday Life.* Chicago, Ill.: Loyola Press, 1999.

Simpson, Ray. *The Celtic Prayer Book* Vol. 1. Stowmarket: Kevin Mayhew, 2003.

Simpson, Ray. *Celtic Prayers for Life Today.* Stowmarket: Kevin Mayhew, 2006.

Sittser, Gerald L. *A Grace Disguised: How the Soul Grows Through Loss.* Grand Rapids: Zondervan, 1996.

Taylor, Charles. *A Secular Age.* Cambridge, Mass.: Belknap Press of Harvard University Press, 2007.

Terpstra, John. *Skin Boat Acts of Faith and Other Navigations.* Kentville, N.S.: Gaspereau Press, 2009.

Thielike, Helmut. *Life Can Begin Again.* Mount London: James Clarke & Co, 1966.

Vanier, Jean. *Drawn into the Mystery of Jesus.* Ottawa: Novalis, 2004.

Vanier, Jean. *Followers of Jesus.* Toronto: Griffin Press, 1973,1976.

Vanier, Jean. *The Broken Body.* Toronto: Anglican Book Centre, 1988.

Veltri, S.J., John. *Orientations* Vol. 1. Guelph, Ont.: Guelph Centre of Spirituality, 1996–1998.

Veltri, S.J., John. *Orientations* Vol. 2 Guelph, Ont.: Guelph Centre of Spirituality, 1996–1998.

Volf, Miroslav. *After Our Likeness: The Church as the Image of the Trinity.* Grand Rapids, Mich.: William B. Eerdmans, 1998.

Volf, Miroslav. *Exclusion & Embrace: A Theological Exploration of Identity, Otherness and Reconciliation,* Nashville: Abingdon Press, 1996.

von Balthasar, Hans Urs. *Prayer.* San Francisco: Ignatius Press, 1986.

RECOMMENDED READING

Wangerin Jr., Walter. *The Book of God.* Grand Rapids, Mich.: Zondervan, 1996.

ACKNOWLEDGEMENTS

I am grateful to the community of friends known as Touchstone Ministries, particularly those on the board who generously approved my time and freedom to do this work—both the work of Touchstone and the work of the book which emerges from this.

My wife Susan has patiently endured my vocational seren-dipities for over 40 years with love, faith and encouragement to freely explore friendship from the safety of a our own rich marriage.

Special thanks to Tom & Karen McCullough, Derek & Susan Okada, Michael & Janet Wilson, Mike & Karen Wilson and Enid Gebbett (Scotland) who provided great venues for me to write and reflect.

Karen Stiller has been a great encourager and whip-cracker as my editor. I am grateful for her hard work, encouragement to do better and ability to laugh in the process.

My "geezer" companion Ron Nikkel has been a close and valued friend on the exploration of these ideas. His investment in my life is a great treasure.

ABOUT TOUCHSTONE MINISTRIES

Founded in 1984, Touchstone is a loosely linked community of friends whose vocation places them in leadership in business, political, arts and spiritual marketplaces. Women and men explore together Jesus' call to love God with heart, soul, mind and strength. His direction to "love our neighbour as ourselves" helps us explore how those in leadership employ power, money and reputation constructively and with integrity.

There are occasional gatherings in small groups, retreats, forums and dinners to mutually support one another's desire to have their leadership emerge from lives centred in the love of Jesus Christ.

OUR MISSION

Offering, encouraging and teaching friendship in Christ among leaders in the business, political, arts and spiritual marketplaces.